CLASSROOM CREATIVITY

An Idea Book for Religion Teachers

NEW REVISED EDITION

Elizabeth Jeep

A Crossroad Book

THE SEABURY PRESS
New York

1977
The Seabury Press
815 Second Avenue
New York, N.Y. 10017

Printed in the United States of America

Library of Congress Cataloging in Publication Data

Jeep, Elizabeth.
   Classroom creativity.

   "A Crossroad book."
   Bibliography: p.
   1. Christian education--Teaching methods.
I. Title.
BV1534.J4   1977   268'.6   77-24719
ISBN 0-8164-2160-9

CLASSROOM CREATIVITY

CONTENTS

CONTENTS

FOREWORD

This unpretentious book has several things going for it. The ideas here have been tried and have proved to work. They are not costly either of material or of time. Their variety is assorted enough to serve the student in both elementary and high school. They also readily suit a wide range of talents and interests.

Some of the ideas and activities here are familiar. They have already become known through the oldest mass medium, the Grapevine. Others are new. In either case, all teachers should find this book a valuable resource. It's not always easy to remember the vital details of some project you heard about from another teacher or noticed when you visited a local school during its annual Open House. Also, when you feel cornered in class for a fresh idea, you can't depend upon what's current on the Grapevine. It might not be right for your group at the moment. But with Classroom Creativity you'll always have good picking.

In addition to its variety and practicality, Classroom Creativity has something perhaps still more important going for it. That is its mentality. It discourages assembly-line activities and promotes personal expression. It encourages teachers to help children discover life, and what's more, to respond to these discoveries in song and dance, in paintings and projections, in recorded sounds and in silent gestures. So does this book reflect a mentality of celebration.

Classroom Creativity, like much of the current educational resource material, understands that learning is a process. More concretely, it understands this process as more than a student coming to know something. It is equally the process of the student making known what he has found: the process of letting life pass through him, of letting life find expression in him. This process requires that the student have at his disposal many ways in which to express himself.

Classroom Creativity is aware that this process cannot be fulfilled only through verbal expression. However, it does not promote other modes of expression at the expense of words. It does not belittle verbal communication in order to promote currently popular modes. It finds equal delight in an exciting light show and a short story or children's book. It does not fall into the trap of dismissing words as only for those over thirty. It recognizes that teachers and students may have been talking too much and saying too little. Not our use of words, but our poor use of them might have perpetuated what Chesterton describes as the dull Christian: one who has been bored to death by the constant repetition of a story he has never heard.

Classroom Creativity provides teachers with a wealth of ways to enrich the student's modes of self-expression and so come to know that all the world is a Word for him to know and to celebrate.

None of these qualities could surface in this book if the author herself were not one of life's bright celebrations.

Gerard A. Pottebaum

NOTE

This book is the result of the thinking and planning of many teachers of religion who believe that children (and adults) are never so close to discovering God as when they are most creative and most themselves. They are convinced that their best lessons were the ones in which the students became most personally involved and made the greatest contribution. In this period of "generation gap" and "authority crisis" it is increasingly important for teachers to engage their students in a genuine search for meaning, a genuine dialogue. The experiences, suggestions, examples, techniques, and resources discussed in this book are those we have found helpful in moving toward this goal.

Part One of this book lists various experiences and activities in which the teacher of religion can involve his or her students, and through which a fresh way of seeing familiar things, a new understanding or a deeper insight can be developed. Part Two outlines the teacher-oriented materials and audio-visual aids which are most helpful for classroom presentations.

Neither section of this book is exhaustive, but the most common, effective, and practical ideas have been included. A variety of suggestions are given under each heading in order to stimulate the reader's imagination. We hope this book will serve as a useful supplement to whatever curriculum or textbook is used.

The original manuscripts upon which this book is based were compiled under the direction of the Office of Religious Education of the Diocese of Oklahoma City and Tulsa. The persons who have contributed in some way to this book are: Sr. M. Antonine, Ms. Bernarda Sharkey, Rev. Don Brooks, Mrs. B. Burrows, Sr. M. DePorres, Mr. Joseph Dillon, Sr. Mary Helen, Ms. Nancy Hennessy Cooney, Mr. Edward Jeep, Dr. Clare Jones, Mrs. Carmen Kelly, Mrs. Margaret King, Mr. Joseph LaBarge, Mrs. Lynn Moroney, Mrs. Patricia Nall, Sr. Elizabeth Pleas, Mrs. Patti Petersen, Sr. M. Richard, Sr. Rose Michelle, Ms. Sharlene Shoemaker, Sr. M. Stanislaus, Ms. Ann Stegman, Sr. M. Stephanie, Sr. Stephen, and Sr. M. Veronica.

This revised edition contains ideas and suggestions learned from many generous and gifted catechists who wrote to me during the nine years that I edited the "Exchange" column of CATECHIST magazine.

Part I:
ACTIVITIES

PREFACE

The word "activities" is used in a wide sense in this book. It does not mean exclusively, nor even primarily, exterior movement. When you read "activity" here we want you to understand "experience" or "response" or "encounter" or "involvement of the child" or "participation"--that is why we have put quotation marks around the word. Because most manuals entitle a certain portion of the religious lesson "activity" and because it is that portion of the lesson plan which this book is designed to enliven, we have settled on this word. But remember: read "activity," but think: stimulation! involvement! experience! response! LIFE!

    Please do not neglect to read the first chapter. It contains our theology of action. Without it the rest of the book would be only a list of gimmicks.

Chapter 1: THE ABC's OF SELECTING ACTIVITIES

The religion teacher must help his students become "doers of the Word, and not hearers only." In order to bring this about, it is necessary to weave religion lessons around some concrete experience which will help bring the lesson from the realm of theory into the realm of the real. Activities can serve this purpose if they:

> reawaken the memory of a past experience
> > Sample Lesson: Mankind is unable to return to God without the intervention of God's Savior.
> > Sample Activity: Each child describes and/or illustrates a time in his life when he was lost or very frightened.

> are analogous to a religious experience
> > Lesson: Christ calls His apostles.
> > Activity: The teacher calls each child by name. He comes up and joins a circle around her. She touches each one and sends him to tell the good news about Jesus to someone at home.

> are new experiences for children
> > Lesson: Anything on the Old Testament, especially something on the Liturgy.
> > Activity: Visit a synagogue.

Religious activities need to reach the heart of the child and help him assimilate the message of Christ. They should be aimed at helping the child to live a life in accordance with the lesson taught. Though each activity cannot do this in an explicit way, the general orientation of the year should do it.

If the activity is to be a genuine response from the child, a true expression of his understanding or insight, then there must be some freedom in the assignment. (Coloring an outlined picture allows neither freedom nor creativity.) The assignment must also be within his capabilities--what goes over his head will never reach his heart.

Though all our activities can be our prayer to the Father, some are more prayerful than others, and some can become more prayerful if we help create the proper atmosphere.

> (Instead of simply demonstrating the administration of a sacrament, for example, one can plan the demonstration as a Bible vigil or "celebration"; if it is baptism, for instance, the children might end with the renewal of their baptismal promises.)

Those activities are also most desirable which draw the children to Christian action in the world.

Activities must also be interesting and varied, or they will not stimulate the children to self-activity, but merely to a bored carrying out of directions. The exterior actions are designed to awaken interior action.
Every teacher knows that children (and adults) learn by doing, and so every teacher weaves some physical and mental exercises into her lesson plans. The religion class is no exception and every manual lists some variety of activities for the teacher to use with her children. Unfortunately, however, many of the suggestions are poor. The activities are above or below the students' level, dull, repetitious, uninspired or useless. There are many possible activities for each lesson, but not all are equally worthwhile. If the experience is meant to satisfy a genuine educational role and not merely to entertain the student or break the monotony of the teacher's voice, then every teacher must develop a good sense of judgment and selectivity in preparing his lesson plans. A good teacher also knows when to branch out from his manual and try to discover new religious activities to bring into the classroom--activities which are . . .

A . . . theologically sound

B . . . educationally valuable

C . . . artistically stimulating

A. "ACTIVITIES" which are theologically sound

The activity, as well as the lesson itself, should always emphasize the essential theological meanings before dwelling on details. Young children tend to notice and remember the anecdotal details of Bible stories (e.g. the seven-day pattern of the creation story), and therefore activities should focus their attention on the religious import of the story. Instead of having the children draw a series of seven pictures showing the "stages" of creation, for instance, it might be better to ask them to draw one large mural portraying some of the wonders God has put in this world, adding the words ". . . and God saw that it was good!"
When learning about liturgy it is good for the children to discuss their religious reality and meaning before dwelling at length on the sacramental signs and essential rites. Likewise, it is good to consider the real meaning of worship (why do we need to pray, why do we need to get together to pray, how did Jesus feel about communal worship with his apostles, etc.) before discussing particular forms of worship (baptism, the Eucharistic meal). Last of all should come an examination of the ritual itself--rubrics, vestments, individual prayers, and so forth.

8

It is recommended that a teacher read at least one good work by a contemporary theologian or Scripture scholar on the main theme of the year in order that he or she be able to draw upon the research and insight of someone with authority in the field. Always currently available are valuable short articles in <u>The Bible Today</u>, <u>Interaction</u>, <u>Liturgy</u>, <u>The Living Light</u>, and <u>Worship</u>. Good articles with many practical suggestions on the teaching of religion are published in <u>The Catechist</u>, <u>The Religion Teachers' Journal</u>, <u>Media & Methods</u>, and <u>Colloquy</u>.

The field of religious education is blossoming with publications, with new books, magazines and other materials coming out constantly. One good way of keeping up-to-date on the latest and best is to read regularly the reviews of new books in the journals mentioned above, and to put your name on various publishers' mailing lists. You may also want to discuss certain ideas and publications with your diocesan or parish religious education director.

B.   "ACTIVITIES" which are educationally valuable

<u>Good</u> catechetical activities should:

A. <u>deepen the child's understanding</u> or appreciation of the lesson by revealing the concreteness of truth, the personal implications of doctrine, the relevance of religion.

Many activities are enjoyable and practical for classroom use, but actually do no more than review or test the memory.

Lesson: The eight Beatitudes as the New Law of Love.

Activity: Having the children make a list of the Beatitudes would be very poor; it would be better to draw a picture of the exercise of one of them in the everyday life of children their age.

B. <u>demand creative effort</u>. The sensitive teacher says enough to start the children thinking, but not so much that thought is not necessary; leaves enough freedom within the assignment for their initiative and inventiveness, requiring that the students hunt, think, and work.

Lesson: Christ sends His disciples to preach.

Activity: Rather than drawing a picture of the biblical event, each child could imagine being one of the seventy-two and write a letter home telling of his or her feelings and experiences on the journey.

C. <u>require personal expression</u>. The child should interpret and develop, not just repeat, what he has learned; the activity should take him a step beyond where the lecture or discussion left off.

> Lesson: Unity of all persons in Christ, all children of one Father.

> Activity: Instead of merely reminding the children to say the words of the Our Father with greater reverence and consciousness, the teacher can ask them to rewrite that prayer, putting those same ideas in their own words.

D. <u>relate to life outside the classroom</u>. The religion classroom is meant to serve the ministry-life and the worship-life of the student. It is not an end in itself. Students must understand that religion is life, not just knowledge; Christianity is commitment, not routine.

> Lesson: The Church; St. Paul's image of "mystical body of Christ"; Our Lord's image of "vine and branches."

> Activity: The children can study (on their own level) the chief beliefs of religious groups other than their own. Guest ministers of other faiths can talk to them. They can do research and write a paper on "beliefs and practices held by Baptists and Catholics (for example) in common." They can write a prayer or design a prayer service for Christian unity.

E. <u>employ as much of the total child as possible</u>.

> Asking children to fill in the blanks in their texts challenges only the memory, and occasionally the intelligence. Ask them to look for magazine pictures which illustrate the application of the lesson just taught, and make posters or decorate a bulletin board with these pictures.

F. <u>correlate with natural interests</u>--those typical of the age level, social background, and I.Q. of the children.

> Eighth-graders do not want to give informal dramatizations of biblical events, though first-graders do; eighth-graders would prefer to act out an argument between a teenager and a parent, and then discuss possible solutions to the conflict between them.

BE SELECTIVE!

is it <u>integral</u> to the lesson?

is it right for <u>these students</u>?

is it <u>worth doing</u>?

C.   "ACTIVITIES" which are artistically stimulating

A.   Freedom is an essential ingredient of creativity. The art which
children produce does not need to be realistic; it does not need to
conform to the teacher's taste. The essence of art is self-expression,
within the discipline imposed by the art medium. There is no place
either in art or in religion for stereotyped patterns. To spend time
tracing around a pattern of a turkey at Thanksgiving, or a "Baby Jesus"
at Christmas, is not a meaningful experience for the child, and it
teaches him nothing of the true meaning of the feast. Such activities
are only busy-work which adults have invented for bored children.

B.   Variety stimulates the children and keeps them challenged to interpret
and express their ideas and feelings in new ways. Variation is necessary in media, subject, material, and motivation.

C.   Color and line and shape and pattern can be used for their aesthetic
and/or emotional value. Yellow, for example, usually conveys joy,
light, and glory, and therefore is useful for resurrection themes.
A jagged line is nervous and tense, a triangular shape is restful and
peaceful looking. Children who are constantly reminded to use colors
and figures only as they are found in nature ("Why don't you make the
tree green, George, instead of orange?" "I think the sheep in your
picture are too large for the shepherd you have drawn.") will never
learn to explore the potential that color and proportion and so forth
have for expressing inner meaning or emotion. Such children sometimes
lose their interest in art because they cannot reproduce things "realistically."

D.   Presentation of an activity:

    (1)   give a clear, precise assignment;
    (2)   in a few words motivate them to do it well--give them the
          spiritual orientation with which they must approach their
          activity;
    (3)   make it attractive and appealing--they should enjoy doing
          it;
    (4)   maintain a purposeful atmosphere--peaceful if it is quiet
          work, orderliness if it is active--activity that gets so
          loud that it destroys the possibility of accomplishing
          the task is frustrating to both teacher and student;
    (5)   give continuous encouragement--especially to the very young
          --be interested in the finished product (encourage and
          commend even the most primitive creations).

E. Exploit the full potential of each activity.

> For example, draw pictures of children carrying out
> one of the beatitudes--when finished don't just post
> them, but compare, discuss, make an album, show and
> explain them to another class, bring them in an
> offertory procession.

> This is a great discipline for the teacher. It
> requires advanced preparation, brings about a con-
> tinuity for the child, makes younger ones more secure,
> and leads the child to respect his work more.

The more useful the better.

> For example, ask older children who are studying the
> words of Christ to make a series of banners with those
> words on them; these may then be used as visual aids
> for younger children, or they could be posted in the
> auditorium for parents' night, or be used in an offer-
> tory procession.

The more prayerful the better.

> For example, after children finish their drawings
> they might write a personal prayer on them or each
> could bring his picture in procession to the front
> of the room or to the Bible stand and leave his
> picture there beside the Bible, and sing an appro-
> priate hymn.

F. Don't get carried away.

> It is possible to focus so much attention on the art
> medium, or on the sophistication of the completed
> project, that the religious meaning of the activity
> is submerged--or lost altogether!

Chapter 2: MUSIC

St. Paul believed that music is a very important part of worship. In his letter to the Christians of Ephesus he wrote, "be filled with the Spirit, speaking to one another in psalms and hymns and spiritual songs, singing and making melody in your hearts to the Lord" (Eph. 5:19-20). St. Augustine taught that "he who sings prayer, prays double." Children, too, love music. Unless they have been led to feel self-conscious or inadequate at it, they find singing a spontaneous, joyous, sometimes even powerful experience, into which they put their hearts, minds and bodies.

The pleasure of singing also comes from the fact that it is conducive to group participation, and helps to create a community atmosphere. Music draws upon and deepens a common attitude or idea and the attitude is then doubly shared. This explains the essential role that liturgical music plays in the life of the Church.

For a well-rounded development, the child's experience should include singing, listening, playing simple instruments (bongo drums, cymbals, etc.) and rhythmic body movement.

IF YOU AND YOUR STUDENTS APPRECIATE MUSIC AND SING OFTEN AND WELL, THEN SKIP THE FOLLOWING ARTICLE AND READ "SOURCES OF SONGS USEFUL IN TEACHING RELIGION."

However, if you are a teacher whose repertoire consists of "Holy God We Praise Thy Name" and a few Christmas carols; if you can never find an adequate note to begin a song, nor suitable ones to continue it once begun; or if you cannot even learn the antiphons to a Gelineau psalm--then you are invited to read on.

It is unnecessary to do without the benefits of music just because you can't sing. You can lead your children to as great an appreciation of and delight in music as any other teacher. All you need is a little more courage, a little more technical assistance, and a little more conviction that it IS worth the extra effort.

IS IT REALLY WORTH THE EFFORT?

Music has always touched the heart as well as the mind of man. It can express or create a mood; it can communicate an insight that cannot be captured by merely spoken words. Music can awaken; it can enchant; it can clothe truth with beauty; it can whisper of inner meaning and inexpressible mystery. Man has always known this. He has used music at all the moving occasions of his life--at his births and deaths, at his marriages and festivals--and especially at his religious rites. He has chosen it, through the centuries, as a vehicle to express his deepest yearnings for God, his thanksgiving to him for abundant harvest--and for the gift of life itself.

The Church knows this. In her Constitution on the Sacred Liturgy, she calls music a necessary and integral part of the solemn liturgy, adding delight to prayer, fostering unity of minds, and conferring greater solemnity upon the sacred rites (see article 112).

Music, then, can help the teacher who wishes to reach the "heart" of the student with God's message, and to awaken some responding echo there. My affirmation that "God is great, God is powerful," can evoke an assent from my children, but a prayerful singing of "A Mighty Fortress Is Our God" is far more likely to stir them to enthusiasm and commitment. Children-- all people--need to express themselves in song to their Creator. We do not want to listen to the choir praise God, each of us must join the hymn. The Council Fathers urge pastors to "ensure that, whenever the sacred action is to be celebrated with song, the whole body of the faithful may be able to contribute that active participation which is rightly theirs . . ." (article 114). Religious singing by the people, in fact, is to be "skill-fully fostered, so that . . . during liturgical services, the voices of the faithful may ring out . . ." (article 118).

Some of us, raised in the days of the "quiet Mass," have found it diffi-cult, if not traumatic, to sing out in Church. But the children we are teaching will find it as natural to praise their Lord together in song, as it is to sing carols around the Christmas tree. Habit will make it a familiar part of Church etiquette, but habit might turn it into meaningless conformity. If we want our children to find in music a means of real prayer, we must do more in our classroom than practice a few basic hymns. We must establish an atmosphere in which singing is easy, joyous, almost spontaneous --as commonplace as drawing or writing. But that is precisely the problem! How can a teacher who cannot sing bring a class to musical life?

STEP 1: LEARN SOME SINGABLE SONGS

There are many sources available to you. You will need the hymnal used in your parish, of course, and one or two others, such as the New People's Hymnal (World Library of Sacred Music, latest and most comprehensive), and Hymnal for Young Christians (F.E.L. Publications). New music is published every day, so watch for it. The diocesan Office of Religious Education or Liturgical Commission will be able to help you. Your fellow teachers can help you too. Organize a beer and pizza "hymnanny" some evening and restock your repertoire. Then go off in the woods and practice these songs to gain confidence.

Since it is easier to teach a song if you have a recording, the parish should have a library of records such as those listed at the end of this chapter. Do not forget popular folksongs and freedom songs--some are as truly religious and far more authentic than many of the hymns we are accus-tomed to.

There are also some records that you will want your children to just listen to, such as the Missa Lubba, or hymns from the Jewish Seder Service.

When a record is not available, a group of older children, talented friends, or the parish choir will be delighted to make a tape recording of the hymns you want to use in class. If someone can add a guitar or piano accompaniment, so much the better. (Be sure the microphone is closer to the voices than to the instrument.) For a training tape it is wise to have the first verse sung twice without harmony or accompaniment, then the complications can be added to the following verses. This cuts down on rewinding chores as the children are learning the song.

STEP 2: MAKE A WISE SELECTION

Your children are the key to your choice of music. Racial, cultural, and social background has influenced their taste. A wise teacher respects this, avoiding songs they consider corny and doggedly searching for music that will "reach" them.

An adolescent needs self-confidence and a relaxed atmosphere in order to sing, so introduce music into your lessons gradually, allowing a group spirit to mature among them. Ask an experienced music teacher what they should be capable of learning, then discover by trial and error what they respond to. Students will generally know if a song is too difficult, and if enough veto it, capitulate gracefully.

Your selection should, of course, be geared to the liturgical season and/ or the doctrinal content of your lesson. It is meant to be an integral part of the learning process, not a break in the classroom routine or singing practice for the Sunday liturgy.

STEP 3: PRESENT THE SONG

Take time to talk about your song--its spirit, mood, doctrinal content, devotional emphasis. If your selection is a psalm, discuss its scriptural vocabulary or images. This discussion is of utmost importance if it is ever going to become meaningful to the student. Teenagers seldom ponder--or even notice--the lyrics of popular songs. They are captured rather by the beat-- the "teen sound." Therefore, do not neglect this introduction to the "message" of the song.

Then you come to the difficult part--teaching the melody. Here <u>you will probably need some technical assistance.</u>

Any music methods book can give you the general procedures such as: play it all the way through first, then teach it phrase by phrase; don't slow it down during the learning phase or they will never sing at the proper tempo.

But people are the best help of all. If you have a teacher's assistant or willing friend, turn this part of the lesson over to him. Combine several classes for specific projects, and teach as a team--"You lead the singing and I'll organize the activity period." Some schools have a specialist visit the classes periodically to add polish to the singing. (Music should not be taught regularly in a separate session, however, or it will become isolated from the rest of the catechetical program.) It is possible to have older children teach a new song, and even better to used talented children in your own class. You can also send copies of a song home occasionally, for the parents to teach.

If you lack personnel, there are always mechanical helpers available. Besides the trusty phonograph and tape recorder, you can experiment with a pitch pipe, or learn a few strategic notes on the piano (if one is available).

REMEMBER! It always sounds 100% better the second day you try it, so don't give up! You will want to practice it several times before assigning it to the category to "usable songs."

STEP 4: LET THE SONG TEACH FOR YOU

Music is versatile, lending itself to a variety of situations. Choose one
to create a mood--reverence, or penitence, or lively rejoicing. Use one
for prayer at the beginning or end of class, at some solemn moment in the
religion period, or as the children's response to God's Word in a Bible
vigil or "celebration." It can be a theme linking several lessons into
one unit. It can (most important) be used in the celebration of Mass,
unifying the child's liturgical life and his learned religion.

Ask the children to write new verses for a hymn, or express its meaning
with gestures or interpretive dance. For homework, ask them to bring in
the record or sheet music of a popular song which has some religious relevance, or which could be evaluated in the light of the topic you are
studying.

Wonderfully creative lessons can be woven around an instrumental record.
When studying baptism, for instance, talk about water--its strength and
universality, its destructive and creative powers, the awe man has always
had for the ocean--the fittingness of this as the sign of our regeneration.
Then play Victory at Sea, telling them to picture in their imaginations the
moods of the sea that the music describes. Give them each a large (LARGE!)
piece of paper and lots of paint--play the record again and let them paint
what the record "says" to them. The fact that this sort of creative teaching is so seldom done is an indication of just how needed it is. We have
almost lost touch with the language of sign and symbol.

STEP 5: DO NEW THINGS

If there is no song "just right" for your lesson, just write one of your own,
or have the children write their own.

For instance:

            "We are all the Lord's apostles, apostles, apostles,
            We are all the Lord's apostles,
            We tell His good news!

            "We tell that He made us.
            He loves us and saved us.
            He is risen, and He lives now!
            The Lord is our King."

            New words written by the teacher of a first-grade class that was
            studying the commission of Jesus to his apostles to go, there-
            fore, and teach . . .

            To be sung to the tune of "Did You Ever See a Lassie."

16

"Take care to wonder at the
world through which you wander.
Never hurry by an open door.
For you live in a universe full of
miracles galore.

"Look for God in good things,
a new born babe that was saved from death.
Praise Him whenever you find Him in anything good.

"Look for God in strange things,
a burning bush or food sent from heaven,
Praise Him whenever you find Him in anything strange.

"Look for God in dry things,
desert sands or a throat that's parched.
Praise Him whenever you find Him in anything dry.

"Look for God in cool things.
Clear spring water or bread from heaven.
Praise Him whenever you find Him in anything cool.

"Look for God in new things.
A promised land and His constant care.
Praise Him whenever you find Him in anything new.

"Look for God in gay things.
Being saved and being free.
Praise Him whenever you find Him in anything gay."

 New words written by a fifth-grade class that was studying
Moses and the Exodus.

To be sung to the tune of "The Wonderful World." The chorus
is unchanged.

HAVE COURAGE, FRIEND!

Does this seem beyond you? You would be surprised how easy it can be.
Perhaps, though, you may want to proceed cautiously until you develop
confidence in your capabilities and the students' response. Fine--but
remember, an inexperienced teacher who is afraid to <u>TRY</u> anything new will
still be inexperienced after years of teaching.
    Begin with honesty, and your battle is half won. Talk to the students
about music; do they like to sing? what are their preferences? what is
their favorite church music? do any of them have special talent or training?

Be frank--"I can't sing very well, so we will have to work together if we are going to be able to enjoy music in our class." This approach has the added benefit of placing more responsibility on the students and encouraging their initiative.

So make up your mind to TRY, with humility and conviction, and willingness to experiment and learn. In this way you can become another Christ, "loosening the tongues" of your students, giving them a voice with which to praise and glorify God, just as the mute man in the Gospel.

SOURCES OF SONGS USEFUL IN TEACHING RELIGION

> Addresses of music publishers are listed
> at the end of this bibliography.

Books and Hymnals:

New Peoples' Hymnal and The People's Mass Book, World Library Publica-
    tions.

Hymnal for Young Christians, Vols. I, II, and III, F.E.L. Publications, Ltd.

Dimension in Song, Paulist Publications.

Journey To Freedom: A Casebook with Music, Swallow Press, 1969.

Young People's Folk Hymnal, Vols. I and II, World Library Publications.

A Treasury of Christmas Songs & Carols, Henry Simon ed., Houghton
    Mifflin, 1973.

The Catholic Book of Worship, Toronto: Canadian Catholic Conference, 1972.

Albums

In most cases both record (or cassette) and score are available.

A CHILD IS BORN, Lucien Deiss, W.L.P.
A NEW DAY, Joe Wise, W.L.P.
A MOUNTAIN MASS, Barry, W.L.P.
A PLACE OF OUR OWN, Misterogers, Small World Enterprises.

A TIME TO KEEP, Howard Bellson, W.L.P.
ACCENT ON YOUTH, Mercury Records. (Especially the song, "Thank You".)
ALIVE IN CHRIST, Lou Fortunate, Sadlier. (Music selections for upper
    elementary texts.)
ALLE, ALLE, Jack Miffleton, W.L.P.

ALLELU! Ray Repp, F.E.L.
AN AMERICAN MASS PROGRAM, Clarence Rivers, W.L.P.
BECOMING ONE, Mission Singers, Avant Garde.
BLESS THE LORD, Bob Hurd, F.E.L.

BUILDING THE EARTH, Sandi Yonikus, Liturgical Press.
CLOSE YOUR EYES, I'VE GOT A SURPRISE, Joe Wise, North American Liturgy
    Resources.
COME ALIVE, Ray Repp, F.E.L.
COME OUT!, Neil Blunt and Jack Miffleton, W.L.P.

COME TO THE FATHER, Paulist Press. (Music selections for 1st grade text.)
EVEN A WORM, Elizabeth Blandford and Jack Miffleton, W.L.P.
FOLLOW ME, John & Amanda Ylvisaker, Vanguard.
FROM EARTHENWARE JUGS, Jack Miffleton, W.L.P.

FUNERAL FOLK MASS, Ian Mitchell, F.E.L.
GATHERED IN LOVE, Paulist Press. (Music selections for 3rd grade text.)
GLAD SONGS! GLAD DAYS!, Mine Publications.
GOD'S PEOPLE, Sadlier. (Music selections for 6th grade text.)

GODSPELL, Stephen Schwartz, Bell Records.
GONNA SING, MY LORD, Joe Wise, W.L.P.
GO TELL EVERYONE, Sacred Heart Choir, Gregorian Institute of America.
GREAT THINGS HAPPEN, Carey Landry, N.A.L.R.

HAND IN HAND, Joe Wise, W.L.P.
HAPPY THE MAN, Sebastian Temple, W.L.P.
HE'S GOT THE WHOLE WORLD IN HIS HANDS AND 18 OTHER SPIRITUALS, RCA Victor.
HI GOD! Carey Landry, N.A.L.R.

IF WE SAW HIM..., Angel Tucciarone, W.L.P.
I KNOW THE SECRET, Medical Mission Sisters, Vanguard.
IN LOVE, Medical Mission Sisters, Vanguard.
IN THE WIND, Peter, Paul and Mary, Warner Brothers Record.

JOIN HANDS, MY BROTHERS, Gregory Miller, W.L.P.
JOY IS LIKE THE RAIN, Medical Mission Sisters, Vanguard.
JOY OF OUR YOUTH, Robert Schaffer, W.L.P.
KEEP IN MIND, Lucien Deiss, W.L.P.

KEEP THE RUMOR GOING, Robert Edwin, Vanguard.
KNOCK, KNOCK, Medical Mission Sisters, Vanguard.
LET ALL THE EARTH SING HIS PRAISE, Tom Parker, W.L.P.
LET GOD'S CHILDREN SING, Lucien Deiss, W.L.P.

LET'S BE TOGETHER TODAY, Misterogers, Columbia Records or Small World
    Enterprises.
LIFE, LOVE, JOY, Silver Burdett Records. (Music selections for grades 1
    through 5; separate records.)
LIKE OLIVE BRANCHES, BIBLICAL HYMNS & SONGS, Lucien Deiss, W.L.P.
MASS FOR YOUNG AMERICANS, Ray Repp, F.E.L.

MEET THE PROPHETS, George Montague, Argus.
MEN OF THE OLD TESTAMENT, George Montague, F.E.L.
MISSA CRIOLA, W.L.P.
MISSA LUBA, W.L.P.

MY LORD, WHAT A MORNING, RCA Victor Record.
NO TIME LIKE THE PRESENT, Jack Miffleton, W.L.P.
O LET HIM IN, Bob Hurd, F.E.L.
ONE IN CHRIST, Sadlier. (Music selections for 5th grade text.)

PSALMS FOR SINGING, S. Somerville, W.L.P.
PURPLE PUZZLE TREE, Concordia Publishing House.
PUT YOUR HAND IN THE HAND, Kama Sutra Records.
RAINBOW SONGS, James Haas, Morehouse-Barlow.

RSVP LET US PRAY!, Medical Mission Sisters, Vanguard.
RUN, COME SEE, Robert Blue, F.E.L.
RUN, LIKE A DEER, Paul Quinlan, F.E.L.
SEASONS, Medical Mission Sisters, Vanguard.

SING FOR JOY, Norman & Margaret Mealy, Seabury Press.
SING! PEOPLE OF GOD, SING!, Sebastian Temple, Franciscan Communications
    Center.
SING PRAISE! SING PRAISE TO GOD!, Ray Repp, F.E.L.
SIX FOLK MASSES FOR AMERICAN YOUTH, W.L.P.

SOME YOUNG CARPENTER, Jack Miffleton, W.L.P.
SONGS FOR CHRIST OUR LIFE, Sadlier. (Music selections for 2nd grade text.)
SONGS FOR JESUS OUR LORD, Sadlier. (Music selections for 3rd grade text.)
SONGS FOR OUR FATHER, Sadlier. (Music selections for 1st grade text.)

SONGS OF GOOD NEWS, W. F. Jabusch, RCA Records and Acta Foundation.
SONGS OF PROMISE, Medical Mission Sisters, Vanguard.
SONGS OF PROTEST AND LOVE, Ian Mitchell, F.E.L.
SONGS OF SALVATION, Sister Germaine, F.E.L.

SONGS OF THE NEW CREATION, The Dameans, F.E.L.
SOULFUL SOUNDS FOR A CHURCH IN CHANGE, The Mission, W.L.P.
SPIRIT, Sadlier. (Music selections for 4th grade text.)
TELL THE WORLD, The Dameans, F.E.L.

THE AMERICAN FOLK-SONG MASS, Ian Mitchell, F.E.L.
THE GELINEAU PSALMS, Gregorian Institute of America.
THE MESSIAH, George Frederick Handel.
THE PROPHET'S DREAM, George Montague and Pat Cunningham, Argus.

THE SPIRT IS A'MOVIN', Carey Landry, N.A.L.R.
THE SOUNDS OF LIFE---CELEBRATING LIFE, Summertime Singers, Sadlier.
THE TIME HAS NOT COME TRUE, Ray Repp, F.E.L.
THE WORLD ABOUT ME, Miriam Rastatter, Alba House.

THERE'LL COME A DAY, Montfort Singers, Alba House.
THEY'LL KNOW WE ARE CHRISTIANS, Peter Scholtes, F.E.L.
UP WITH PEOPLE, Pace Publications.
WALK TO THAT GLORY LAND, The Dameans, F.E.L.

WATCH WITH ME, Joe Wise, N.A.L.R.
WELCOME IN, Joe Wise, N.A.L.R.
WHATSOEVER YOU DO, W. F. Jabusch, Acta Foundation.
WITH JOYFUL LIPS, Lucien Deiss, W.L.P.

WITH SKINS AND STEEL, Jack Miffleton, W.L.P.
WON'T YOU BE MY NEIGHBOR? Misterogers, Small World Enterprises.
WOMEN OF THE OLD TESTAMENT, Sarah Hershberg, F.E.L.
YES, LORD, Carey Landry, N.A.L.R.

YOU ARE SPECIAL, Misterogers, Small World Enterprises.
YOU'LL NEVER WALK ALONE, The Lettermen, Capitol Records.

Folk and popular songs that lend themselves to religious education are too numerous to list. Your students and the back issues of religious education journals can help you with suggestions.

The following books have excellent bibliographies of musical resources:

Life, Love, Joy teacher's manuals, by Manternach & Pfeifer, Silver Burdett.

Children, Celebrate! Resources for Youth Liturgy. Rabalais & Hall, Paulist Press, 1974.

Come, Be Reconciled, Youth Penance Resources. Rabalais, Hall, & Vavasseur, Paulist Press, 1975.

PUBLISHERS/DISTRIBUTORS OF RELIGIOUS MUSIC

Acta Foundation
    4848 N. Clark Street, Chicago, Illinois 60640

Agape
    Carol Stream, Illinois 60187

Alba House
    Canfield, Ohio 44406

Argus Communications
    3505 N. Ashland Avenue, Chicago, Illinois 60657

Avant Garde
    250 West 57th Street, New York, New York 10019

Bell Records
    1776 Broadway, New York, New York 10019

Capitol Records, Inc.
    1750 N. Vine Street, Hollywood, California 90028

Concordia Publishing House
    3558 S. Jefferson Avenue, St. Louis, Missouri 63118

F.E.L. Publications
    1925 Pontius Avenue, Los Angeles, California 90025

Franciscan Communications Center
    1229 S. Santee Street, Los Angeles, California 90015

Gregorian Institute of America (G.I.A. Publications, Inc.)
    7404 S. Mason Avenue, Chicago, Illinois 60638

Houghton Mifflin
    2 Park Street, Boston, Massachusetts

Kama Sutra Records, Inc.
    810 Seventh Avenue, New York, New York 10019

Liturgical Press
    Collegeville, Minnesota 56321

Mercury Records
    One IBM Plaza, Chicago, Illinois 60611

MINE Publications
    25 Groveland Terrace, Minneapolis, Minnesota 55403

Morehouse-Barlow
    14 East 41st Street, New York, New York 10017

North American Liturgy Resources
    300 East McMillan Street, Cincinnati, Ohio 45219

Pace
    810 Seventh Avenue, New York, New York 10019

Paulist Press
    400 Sette Drive, Paramus, New Jersey 07652

RCA Victor Records
    1133 Avenue of the Americas, New York, New York 10013

William H. Sadlier Co.
    11 Park Place, New York, New York 10007

Seabury Press, Inc.
    815 Second Avenue, New York, New York 10017

Silver Burdett Co.
    250 James Street, Morristown, New Jersey 07960

Small World Enterprises, Inc.
    1 Palmer Square, Room 435, Princeton, New Jersey 08540

Swallow Press
    811 West Junior Terrace, Chicago, Illinois 60613

Vanguard Music Corp.
    250 West 57th Street, New York, New York 10019

Warner Brothers Records
    3300 Warner Blvd., Burbank, California 91510

World Library Publications (formerly World Library of Sacred Music)
    2145 Central Parkway, Cincinnati, Ohio 45214

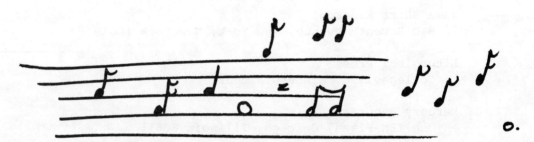

Chapter 3: GESTURE

"Now thank we all our God   * raise arms.

with heart and hands and voices   * touch heart with both
                                               hands, then hold them
                                               forward with palms out-
                                               ward, then cup them
                                               around mouth.

who wondrous things hath done   * describe a large circle
                                               with hands.

in whom this world rejoices;   * wave and shake hands, as
                                               though cheering and jump
                                               up and down.

Who from our mother's arms   * move arms as though
                                               rocking a baby.

hath blessed us on our way   * make large cross with
                                               right hand.

with countless gifts of love,   * raise arms, flutter
                                               hands and fingers, and
                                               slowly lower hands all
                                               the way to floor.

and still is ours today."   * stand again, fold arms
                                               across chest.

(People's Mass Book, World Library Publications,
    p. 257. Used with permission of the publisher.)

The simple gestures described above were designed by a third-grade class, to be used in a special celebration of the Eucharist. They first discussed the meaning of the hymn, and learned to sing it. Then they were asked to "sing the song with their bodies," showing everyone who saw them that they understood what it meant and felt like to thank God. They they took each phrase in turn, suggested and tried out several possible gestures, and selected the one they liked best. When the song was "choreographed" they practiced until the gestures flowed smoothly and gracefully, in synchronization with the words and rhythm of the song.

Is this just a teacher's gimmick? A pleasant change of routine for the children? It can be only that. But, with proper development, it can be much more. Physical gesture, just like spoken words, have sacramental ability to deepen an emotion, to lift one's spirits, to communicate a feeling to another person. A kiss, for instance, is a way people have of sharing love, but in the sharing the love is deepened. So too, carrying gifts to the altar in an offertory procession can make more conscious and more real the self-giving it symbolizes. Sorrow, joy, fear, thanksgiving, petition, offering, receiving, love, hatred, loneliness, and unity are only a few of the universally experienced human responses which come under discussion in religion classes.

Some ritualized actions are so universally understood and used that men forget that they are really a form of liturgy--a handshake, a toast, a birthday party. By including both "religious" and "secular" rituals in the religion class we can help the children learn to express their deep feelings, and to express themselves as part of a group. And we help them learn to read the language of the symbolic actions of the liturgy.

The use of gestures to accompany a reading or song comes easily for a young child, but can also be used in the upper grades. It is good "warm-up" activity by children who are still too shy for regular dramatizations. Since all the children can participate equally and simultaneously it has an advantage over drama.

The older children will take this activity as seriously as the teacher. The teacher who really --deep down-- considers it awkward or childish, will communicate this feeling to the students no matter how much she tries to get them interested.

For Instance:

CALMING THE STORM

Read the calming of the storm from Matthew 8:23-27 (or other event, parable, psalm, etc.) and ask the children how they would feel when the storm came up and the boat began to rock. Ask them to show that emotion in their faces, and to rock in their seats as though they were in the boat. Would they be mad at Jesus if He just kept on sleeping? Would they be

afraid that He would be washed overboard if He didn't wake
up and hang on to something? Ask them to shake Him and
wake Him up; to act then as Jesus would--is He calm or
worried? What does He do? Now they are the apostles
again--how do they feel, what do they think, and so on.

   Finally, re-read the passage slowly, allowing them to
"act it out" as they go.

Another Example:

   Lessons on the eucharist should include some kind of simple
   ceremony which features bread. It should be a form of
   bread which is recognizable to the children (as distinct
   from "communion bread") such as an uncut loaf or home-
   baked rolls. These should be placed on a table with a
   linen cloth and candles, or in the center of a circle of
   children. A reading or hymn can be included in the ceremony, but the important ritual is for the children to break
   the bread and pass it around the circle with a solemn gesture of offering, saying, "Be my friend. Share my bread."

   The more extensive a teacher's "vocabulary" of gestures and signs, the
more helpful he or she will be to the students. Notice the positions by
which dancers express sorrow, terror, love, companionship, reconciliation,
indecision. How are natural gestures exaggerated for dramatic effect?
Why do the gestures seem more effective if the actor/dancer is moving about
in space rather than standing still? How do the liturgical ministers of
your church execute the ritual gestures assigned to them? How can a transition be made from one gesture to another so as to avoid an awkward pause?
Practice some gestures before your mirror and repeat them until they become
graceful, comfortable and prayerful. Start with some you already use (perhaps without being aware of them as "gestures") such as approaching someone
to shake hands, opening a door and welcoming a person in, hailing a taxi,
waving to a friend across the street, tip-toeing, beckoning, hugging.
   To pursue this topic further, read the chapters in this book on dance
and drama, activities that are closely related to gesture.

"One of the most startling discoveries I made,
I think it was in high school, all of a sudden
it just hit me that you could learn outside of
school. I was never really taught that this
was true and this kind of blew my universe wide
open."

> College Dropout, 4.0 average

"I've sat through dozens of boring
lectures and it always makes me wonder
whether maybe I'll wake up some morning
and find myself ensconced in apathy
with all my ideas and ideals vanished.
Teachers of America, you are not being
paid to babysit but to stimulate. If
that's too demanding, don't tamper with
my life anymore."

> Marion Ostruske, high-school student

"Perhaps a school's greatest contribution is that
it teaches patience, forbearance and the ability
to survive in a situation which is generally absurd.
If this is true, perhaps we are being prepared for
life."

> D. L., high-school student

Chapter 4: DANCE

Dance is a very enjoyable activity and can be a useful tool for the children to use in interpreting visually a situation, feeling, biblical scene, and so forth. It is very much akin to drama, and many of the same teaching and motivating principles apply. If a group is too shy to dance, the teacher can draw them into trying out bodily gestures gradually. After they are at ease with that, they will be more able to dance freely.

For Instance:

AN EASTER DANCE

A first-grade class, under the direction of Sister Mary Stanislaus, S.C.L., developed an informal dance as an interpretation of the resurrection. It was developed over the course of several weeks. Sister Mary Stanislaus began by telling the story of the resurrection in her own words, reading short sentences or phrases from the Bible. She led them to a discussion of the event, helping them to put it in their own words, and focusing their attention on the meaning of the resurrection to the people involved. "How do you think Mary felt? How did the apostles feel when they realized that Jesus had not left them forever? How did Mary Magdalen feel before she saw Jesus in the garden? after?" Sister then suggested that they act out the scenes, again focusing their attention on the meaning of the resurrection by asking questions: "How can we make ourselves a part of the resurrection of Jesus? How can we learn from this dramatization and enjoy being part of His new life?" As children volunteered to take various parts (Sister never forces a child) and began to work it out, Sister played a classical record for background music. Impressed by the music, one girl suggested that it would be better to dance the scene. They all removed their shoes and practiced a few basic ballet steps (VERY basic, says Sister Stanislaus) and, because of the natural spontaneity of young children, they were soon able to dance around the room, more or less gracefully, in rhythm with the music.

At another time, the class wrote a narration for their "happening." The children told Sister what to write and she copied it down just as they dictated. As she read it back they polished it and added details.

Later the children volunteered to take various parts, with the bulk of the class acting as Holy Women, crowds, and so on--with everyone participating.

The children suggested staging effects such as having the narrator stand on the bookcase for dramatic emphasis. Mary's veil and Christ's tunic were the only costumes, and the scene opened with Jesus hidden under a sheet (the tomb) which He threw off.

Because of the naturalness and seriousness with which Sister approached the celebration, the children enjoyed the experience, and absorbed some of the meaning and joy of Easter from it. They were surprised and delighted that other teachers and some parents wanted to see their dramatic dance, and were very unaffected in their presentation of it to "outsiders."

Many occasions for short, spontaneous dances will arise during the year. After telling the story of Jesus curing the blind man or the paralytic, for example, the children might enjoy expressing in dance the delight of the cured person at being able to see all the things around him, or at being able to exercise his muscles and limbs for the first time. Prepare the children by talking about the feelings and actions of the person. "What would you notice first? Would you move quickly or slowly? Would you pick up things and handle them gently and hold them close to your eyes? How would you move to the next thing that you noticed? How would you react to friends you could see for the first time? Would you (the ex-paralytic) walk stiffly at first? Would you run, skip, touch your toes, turn a somersault?

Some background music is essential. Removing the shoes increases the freedom and "grace" of movements, and reminds the children that their actions should be dance-like. You might wish to narrate the dance as it progresses, "talking the children along" unobtrusively. Close by drawing the dancers to a circle where they offer thanks to God for His power and end in a deep reverential bow.

On other occasions the whole lesson or celebration can be built around a dance. This example is taken from CELEBRATE SUMMER! A GUIDEBOOK FOR CONGREGATIONS, E. M. Jeep and G. Huck (Paulist).

"This liturgy celebrates the family of all the earth. It is designed primarily for children, but adults present should actively participate. It needs a large open room (or the outdoors) and a great mixture of supplies for making masks: swatches of fabric, paper bags, cardboard boxes the size of faces, glue, tape, ribbon, staplers, a variety of kinds and colors of paper, paint, felt pens, and any miscellaneous things that can be found. These should be on tables or arranged on the floor for easy access.

"As the people enter they see others already sitting together and singing, perhaps something simple like "Enter, rejoice and come in," Journey to Freedom. When everyone is present a storyteller tells of the American Indian myth: that once the "four-leggeds" and the "two-leggeds" spoke the same language and that the trees and plants sat in the great councils with them. All were brothers and sisters. This is what we want to celebrate. The storyteller has little pieces of paper, as many as there are participants, each with the name of a different creature (fly, tiger, boy, girl, daisy, dandelion, pine tree, rain, sun, fire, soil, cow, dog, tulip, wolf, coyote --as many as are needed). Everybody draws a card and will make that mask. A leader introduces briefly the materials that are available, and says that everyone should explore for a while before beginning. While the work goes on, music might be played. Try Indian music. Two good records are "Sounds of Indian America" on the Indian House label and "American Indian Dances" on Folkways label. When a person is finished, he or she can go and sit down and listen to the music.

"When the group comes back together, all sit in one large circle and each person is given a chance to show his or her mask and identify it. Then the storyteller finishes--with help from this masked council. The men began to kill the animals, the insects brought disease to the men, fire went out of control, rain didn't fall. It is another way of explaining sin and hardship--one that makes a lot of sense. As the different brothers and sisters are mentioned, they can sound off or move about as called for. At the end, all might have their backs turned on one another.

"Now, as a sign of what we are looking for, we dance together, the way it might be if . . . Let the music start, then take someone's hand, ask them to take the next person's. The hora is a good circle dance, but there are others, or a simple step can be invented. A good book for dances is Folk Dancing by Richard Kraus, Macmillan; an RCA Victor record, "All-Purpose Folk Dances" has with it a booklet giving the proper steps. Take enough time to relax so that no one will be worried about joining in. It should be lively, exhausting and a bit hilarious.

"Then the group gathers, sitting close together on the floor, and listens very quietly to Bob Dylan singing "Father of the Night," New Morning album, Columbia Records. A simple cake is shared while all listen. The masks are removed for this. The celebration ends with a prayer of thanksgiving for this family, and the petition that all can learn to live together in peace.

"Another celebration with the same theme, might be built around a good telling of the story of Saint Francis and the wolf of Gubbio. It can be found in any biography of Francis. God's Troubadour by Sophie Jewett, Crowell, is well written. The storyteller should tell it in his or her own words."

This celebration has been quoted at length because it illustrates several important things about the way dance should be used in religious education. First, and most important, the dance is integrated into the event as a whole; it is not a distinct "production." There is no elaborate staging called for, although the masks play an important role in establishing the mood and credibility of the dance itself. Second, the movement of the dance (in this case a circle) is selected because of its appropriateness to the point or message of the celebration (the unity of all created beings). The masks echo the dance rituals of many Indian tribes. This and the music give the event a wholeness and unity of theme and expression which is both artistic and strong. This celebration also illustrates one way in which stories, myths, and art forms other than those found in the Bible can be an authentic source of religious insight for our children (and ourselves!).

RESOURCES

The use of dance in liturgy and prayer is expanding rapidly. For anyone interested in pursuing this subject, and especially for those interested in enlarging their vocabulary of movements and bodily expressions, an excellent guide is LEARNING THROUGH DANCE, Carla De Sola (Paulist). It is well illustrated, and combines theory, procedures and examples of dances based on six themes (communication, freedom, love, life, peace and happiness). While it is intended as a manual for dance class, an individual can learn a great deal from it.

Another resource is DANCE FOR THE LORD (World Library Publications) by Lucien Deiss and Gloria Weyman. The book treats the theological, liturgical and aesthetic aspects of sacred dance, and is illustrated with photos, sketches and music. A cassette of the choreographed songs is also available.

Jack Weiner and John Lidstone have included natural and spontaneously filmed photographs of children in CREATIVE MOVEMENT FOR CHILDREN: A DANCE PROGRAM FOR THE CLASSROOM (Van Nostrand Reinhold Co.), a book which offers ideas for movement and dance within the capability of most classroom teachers.

IN THE CLASSROOM:

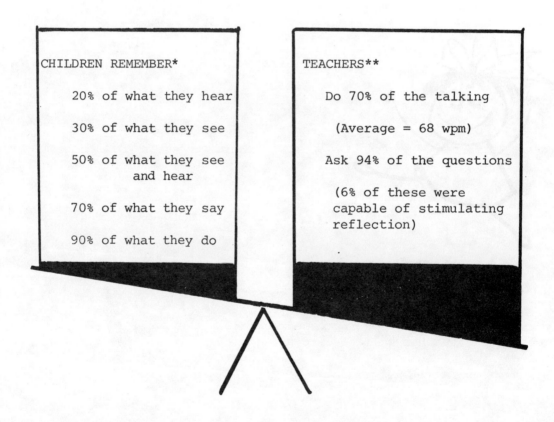

CHILDREN REMEMBER*

    20% of what they hear

    30% of what they see

    50% of what they see
         and hear

    70% of what they say

    90% of what they do

TEACHERS**

    Do 70% of the talking

    (Average = 68 wpm)

    Ask 94% of the questions

    (6% of these were
    capable of stimulating
    reflection)

* Magda Kelber, quoted by L. Zenetti, God's Children Learn in Joy,
       New York: Herder and Herder, 1968.

** Dr. William D. Floyd, "Do Teachers Talk Too Much?" Religion
      Teacher's Journal, January, 1969.

Chapter 5: DRAMA

Drama has played a rich part in the history of the Church. During the middle ages the church buildings themselves were used for the performance of plays based on the events of Scripture (mystery plays), or the lives of the saints (miracle plays), or the Christian virtues as lived out in everyday life (morality plays). The "Passion Play" which is still performed in many places at Eastertime is a direct descendant of these medieval dramas. These activities not only gave people the opportunity of participating in and showing their reverence for the great Christian figures and events, but also showed the importance that those events held. These plays served as a form of religious education at a time when people did not read or write.

Though we can read about these things today, the value of acting them out, the value of putting oneself in another's shoes and discovering how he or she felt is not diminished. For that reason dramatization holds a significant place in catechetics. Dramatization in the religion class is more than just an opportunity for reinforcing the children's understanding of a biblical event. It is an opportunity to express themselves in a given situation as characters in a play, and thus to react in their own way to the lesson or moral which the story or incident contains. Through these experiences they can be helped to make their own personal responses to the world around them, with the Gospel as the source of inspiration.

Dramatics can be very formal, with carefully rehearsed lines, elaborate costumes, and so on, or very informal and spontaneous. The most useful for religious education is the informal type of activity which is more free and unrehearsed, with a minimum of scenery, props, and costumes (just enough to stimulate the imagination), and with no view toward public presentation. Exact outcomes are unpredictable with this kind of drama because the students put more personal interpretation into it.

This activity comes naturally to children, whose lives are filled with "play-acting" or imitations of adult life. But children, especially as they get older, are often inhibited in this activity by the criticism of adults, by social pressure from peers, or by a natural self-consciousness. In order to awaken what is perhaps repressed and allow the children's spontaneity to blossom, the teacher will need to put the children at ease and develop their self-confidence. The children have to overcome conformism and the fear of failure. The more they are able to "be themselves" the more they can "be someone else."

The more the children can identify with the characters they portray and with the conflicts involved in the scene, the more imagination they will bring to the project and the more impact it will make on them. Therefore, it is always advisable to discuss, or in some way present and develop the meaning of the situation to be portrayed before they begin to act it out. Over-discussion can take the freshness and purpose from the activity and leave nothing for the actors to interpret, but they do need some kind of "warm-up" or they will be stiff and non-communicative.

Discuss the story or situation enough for the students to understand the point of it, and the characters involved. Ask questions which will help them to act it out, such as: "How would you feel if you were blind and could not get a job? Have you ever seen a beggar asking for money downtown? How did he do it? From the story does it seem as though Bartimaeus was a calm or excitable person? How would you feel if Jesus gave you sight?" The portrayal of characters will be superficial and stereotyped unless the children are nudged to think beyond the surface of the people and events.

SUGGESTIONS FOR BRINGING CREATIVE DRAMATICS INTO THE RELIGION PROGRAM

> NB: Creative dramatics as described here are not to be confused with paraliturgical celebrations. Both re-enact an event. But in celebration the predominant goal is the evocation of a worshipful response by entering more fully into the mystery. In creative dramatics, the predominant goal is to connect Scripture and life. However, work in dramatics is an excellent help and preparation for classroom celebrations.

PLAN A: As a beginning, let the children agree on a set of gestures to accompany a prayer or poem. Do this several times. (See the chapter in this book on GESTURE.)

Then let them graduate to pantomime, which is acting out a scene without saying anything. Stress group pantomimes in the beginning--all the children doing the same thing at the same time. They do not imitate each other, but each one acts out the theme independently. For example, they could all be the sower scattering his seed, each going about it as he or she thinks best. Or some could be the good seeds, coming up strongly and sturdily, or the seeds blown by the wind, choked by the weeds, and so forth.

Help them develop sensory impressions too. They can be the apostles walking along the dusty roads with Jesus, or being tossed about in the boat, or climbing a hill, or catching fish from the lake (smell the fish, do they wiggle when you load them into the boat?), tasting the loaves and fish.

The children need quite a bit of opportunity to work with feelings and emotions before they attempt characterizations, such as portraying in pantomime the sacrifice of Isaac. The teacher might read the narrative from Scripture as they act it out.

After experiencing success in these two stages, they will be ready to use words with their pantomime, and this becomes drama in the fuller sense.

(This works best with younger children.)

PLAN B: Divide the class into groups (about six per group) and appoint
          a leader to distribute parts. (With first grade it is best
          for the teacher to assign parts in the beginning.)

          Set a time limit of about 10 minutes. This forces the
          children to concentrate on the project at hand, and also
          makes them concentrate on essentials.

          After the presentation the children should discuss what
          they can do next time to make their dramatization better.

PLAN C: "Role playing" or "socio-drama" generally refers to situations
          from ordinary life which children are asked to portray. By
          portraying experiences they have had, it is hoped that children
          will discover other ways to handle situations.

          Ask them to dramatize, for example, a child being unkind
          on the playground. How do the observers react? How does the
          child being bullied react?

          Ask two students to stage an argument and a third to act
          as their mother. (Stop the acting whenever the actors have
          portrayed enough to start discussion--there is no official
          end of the scene with this type of drama.) After the scene
          is finished ask the other students whether they thought the
          "mother" acted in a realistic manner, how they think the
          mother felt, whether she handled her quarrelling children
          well, what they would have done, and so on. (The teacher
          will have to keep urging the children to get beyond the
          superficial, pat answers which are the immediate response
          to a question in religion class.)

Describe a problem situation, ask them how they would solve it, what results would develop from that action, ask them what they would do about the new situation.

PLAN D: The entire class can participate in a dramatic situation.

They can be the Israelites marching through the desert, for example. Everyone gathers in the accustomed room, puts on hats and coats, tiptoes past the sleeping Egyptians (the other classes), following Moses (who has planned the itinerary through the building and out of doors) quickly until they cross the Red Sea (a driveway or other landmark) and then at a more leisurely pace, praying, cheering, singing, complaining to Moses and Aaron about the heat. They could perhaps set up a tent and eat sack lunches together.

PLAN E: A picture can be used as a discussion starter. Behind every picture there is a story: how do you think this situation got started? Where are they going? What do you think will happen next? Why did he do that?

PLAN F: Divide the class into three groups, and ask each to take one aspect of the same selection, that is, history (the past event), mystery (the present reality that the past event points to), and majesty (the future fulfillment of that reality in the kingdom of God).

For example, let the first group dramatize the multiplication of the loaves and the fish (the historical event). Let the second group act out the way in which Christ feeds His people today (in mystery), and let the third group act out the way in which we will be fully satisfied in the final kingdom (majesty).

PLAN G: Dramatize Jesus' parables in contemporary settings. (To help the students recognize the relevance of the Christian message to our times.)

Interpret the story of the Unjust Steward in terms of right-to-work laws, social injustice, labor-management problems.

Interpret the story of the Good Samaritan in terms of racial tensions, liability laws.

PLAN H: Combine puppetry and role-playing. This enables the teacher (behind a puppet) to draw self-conscious children into the activity, and also offers children who are uneasy on an open "stage" something to hide behind and something to do with their hands as they play a part.

For example, students can, with the use of simple hand puppets, act out a scene in which a child's grandfather dies, and various persons (parents, minister, best friend, adult neighbor or relative) comfort and help the family. In this example, the subject is a sensitive one, and the use of puppets might help children show sorrow or ask questions they were not able to manage in real situations within their own families.

BOOKS ON DRAMA

The following are standard texts and have the most complete explanation of the philosophy of creative dramatics, plus helpful practical suggestions.

Batchelder, Marjorie and Comer, Virginia Lee. Puppets and Plays: A Creative Approach. New York: Harper and Bros., 1956.

Burger, Isabel B. Creative Play Acting, 2nd ed. New York: Ronald Press, 1966.

Cheifetz, Dan. Theater in my Head. Boston: Little, Brown & Co., 1971.

Gillies, Emily. Creative Dramatics for All Children. Washington, D.C.: Association for Childhood Education International, 1973.

Heinig, Ruth and Stillwell, Lyda. Creative Dramatics for the Classroom Teacher. Englewood Cliffs, N.J.: Prentice-Hall, 1974.

Naughton, Irene Mary. Make Ready the Way of the Lord. Milwaukee: Bruce Publishing Co. (Dramatic narratives for pantomime and bible plays.)

Siks, Geraldine Brain. Creative Dramatics: An Art for Children. New York: Harper & Bros., 1958.

Waddy, Lawrence. The Bible as Drama. New York: Paulist Press, 1975. (90 bible stories presented as plays.)

Ward, Winifred. Playmaking with Children, 2nd ed. New York: Appleton-Century-Crofts, 1957.

An excellent source for books on creative dramatics is: The Drama Book Shop/ Publishers, 150 West 52nd Street, New York, New York 10019.

SOME GENERAL REMARKS

1. The atmosphere must be comfortable, warm, and accepting in order for the children to feel free to be enthusiastic, and to explore ideas through acting.

2. Timing is important. Don't push the project if the children do not seem to be in the right mood.

3. The story must have inherent dramatic possibilities. The Sermon on the Mount, for example, does not involve action or dialogue.

4. Visual illustrations can "set" the interpretation. It would be mean-ingless, for example, to have them act out the Prodigal Son story if they had just seen it on a film strip.

5. Leave the words and actions to the children's ingenuity. Help them if they get too preoccupied with details.

6. Help them decide on an ending point before they begin. For example, end the return of the Prodigal Son with everyone leaving to go to the banquet.

7. Keep the emphasis on the point of the story rather than just the acting itself.

8. Allow opportunity for all children to take major parts during the year. Children's participation should be encouraged but not forced. Non-speaking parts can be provided for extra-shy students.

9. Children need not "look the part." Why pick the pretty girl instead of the fat one for the part of Our Lady? The point of dramatization is to provide experience in looking beyond the surface. Christians are, after all, committed to the belief that the external is not an accurate gauge of the interior.

10. Help the children put themselves into the part honestly, and with their whole imagination. Say "John, you _be_ the blind man," rather than, "John, you _act like_ the blind man."

11. Background music can often be used to set the right mood for the play.

12. Keep interference to a minimum once the acting has begun. Allow the children their own interpretation. (It is the process, not the product, that is important.) But _do_ keep the play moving.

13. Keep it short.

14. Don't use creative dramatics so often that the students become bored with it.

15. Evaluating a play with the children after it is over will help them improve next time. "How do you think it went? Do you like the way _____ happened? Anything we could have added?

Jose Rodriquez is a quiet, defeated looking Puerto Rican boy, whose name and presence no one remembers. He even put a note in the suggestion box wishing himself a happy birthday. Jose's teacher relates . . .

From Up the Down Staircase by Bel Kaufman. Englewood Cliffs: Prentice-Hall.

"The discussion I started in class--about good intentions and responsibility--proved so lively, that I decided to follow it up with a dramatization. I asked them to come prepared the next day to transform the classroom into a courtroom; we would plead the case, as a sequel to the story. Reminding them to familiarize themselves with the people and the situation in the story and to remain in character during the improvised court session, I assigned the roles: mother, father, neighbor, child, prosecuting attorney, witnesses for the defense and the prosecution, even the doctor. I realized that we had left out the judge. Through one of those swift moments of inspiration, I turned to Jose Rodriquez and asked him to be prepared to act the judge. A few in the class snickered; Jose nodded; and I myself had no idea what to expect.

The following day he appeared in class in a cap and gown--a black graduation gown and mortar-board, borrowed or rented at what trouble or expense I could only guess, and a large hammer for a gavel. He bore a look of such solemn dignity that no one dared to laugh.

He sat at my desk and said: "The court clerk is supposed to say they gotta rise."

There was such authority in his voice that slowly, one by one, the class rose. It was a moment I don't think I will ever forget.

The class was directed to sit down, and the wheels of justice proceeded to turn. The prosecution and the defense testified; witnesses were called, examined, cross-examined; excitement ran high. When anyone spoke out of turn, Jose would pound on the desk with his hammer: "This here court will get quiet. Call the next witness. You keep quiet, or you'll be charged with contempt."

He overruled every objection: "Maybe I'm stup_ed_, but I'm the judge and you gotta listen."

And when Harry Kagan challenged him on court procedure, he said, with quiet assurance: "I ought to know. I been."

The court ruled for the defense.

When the bell rang, Jose slowly removed his cap and gown, folded them neatly over his notebook, and went on to his next class; but he walked as if he were still vested in judicial robes.

I don't think he will ever be quite the same."

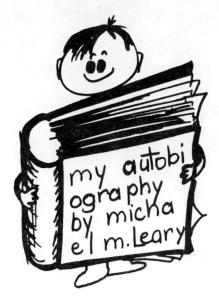

Chapter 6: CREATIVE WRITING

Creative writing may be defined as an imaginative expression of a person's feeling, experiences, or understandings, in either prose or poetry form. It belongs in Christian education classes because:

1. Children will reveal in writing what they would or could never express orally. (The teacher must first gain their confidence so that they are sufficiently at ease to permit a free flow of ideas and thoughts.)

2. Writing helps the teacher know the students better, and communicate with them more realistically.

3. The teacher learns the false impressions students pick up, and can correct them.

4. It gives the students an opportunity for free expression, and encourages them to reflect upon their experiences, their feelings, the mysteries of God's actions, and so on.

5. It encourages children to translate religious truths into familiar terms.

For very young children, or for those who are not used to creative writing, it might be well for the teacher and the class to build a vocabulary of words and phrases related to the topic. These could be written on the board and children would be free to refer to these during the writing period.

BASIC PRINCIPLES: See Wolfe, Don Marion. <u>Language Arts and Life Patterns</u>, <u>Grades 2-8</u>, and <u>Creative Ways to Teach English, Grades 7-12</u>. New York: Odessy Press, 1958.

For Instance:

 1. Compose original prayers, stations of the cross, litanies.

LITANY FOR THE LONELY STUDENTS

For those who are lonely because they have had a fight with their
friends,
        Lord hear our prayer,
                Lord have mercy.

For those who are lonely because they have no brothers or
sisters to play with or share things with,
        Lord hear our prayer,
                Lord have mercy.

For those who are lonely because they are in a new school or
neighborhood,
        Lord hear our prayer,
                Lord have mercy.

For those who are lonely because they aren't included in
a project,
        Lord hear our prayer,
                Lord have mercy.

(from a litany composed by seventh-graders)

2. Rewrite parables in modern terms.

"A man was once on his way down from Mangum to Altus
when he fell into the hands of cotton farmers; they
put him and all of his children to work in the cotton
fields, gave him a very meager wage, and left him to
find another job when the harvesting was finished.
Now one of the priests from Prince of Peace Church
happened to be traveling down the same road, but
when he saw the man in the tin barracks, he passed
by on the other side. If only we could get some anti-
poverty money, he thought, someone could be hired to
help that man.

"In the same way a full colonel who was stationed
at the Air Base saw him, and regretting that he would
probably be transferred soon and so could not help the
man, he passed by on the other side.

"But a communist traveler who came upon him was moved
with compassion when he saw him. He went up and offered
to help the man find a better place to live. He then
lifted them into his own car, and bringing them into
Altus, looked after them. Having called a friend who
ran a lumber yard about a permanent job for the man, he
bought some groceries for the family with his own money,
and leaving $85.00 with the grocer, he arranged that the
man could buy food until he could pay from his own salary.
'Look after him,' he said, 'and on my way back from
Lawton I will make good any extra expense you have.'

"Which of these three, do you think proved himself a
neighbor to the man who fell into the hands of the cotton
farmer?"

"The one who took pity on him," he replied.

Jesus said to him, 'Go, and do the same yourself.'"

(From Luke 10:25-37)

3. Write a haiku (a Japanese poem of three lines, having 5, 7, and 5
syllables respectively).

    God loves Israel
    He led her through the desert
    He gave her life

    Today is desert
    We hunger for new Moses
    and new manna

4. Write a topic poem (a poem of five lines; first line contains only one
word--a noun, the topic of the poem; second line contains two adjectives
relating to the noun; third line three verbs; fourth line a four-word
comment; fifth line a single word which is synonomous with that used in
the first line).

    Kingdom
     Heavenly, earthly
      Grows, reveals, challenges
       The now of our past and future
        Salvation.

Variation A: lines have one, two, three, four, and one words respect-
tively, as above, but the second describes the first, the third and
fourth describe a movement or action, the last is again a single syno-
nym.

45

```
Christ
  God's Son
    Born in Bethlehem
      Savior of all people
        Lord
```

(by a sixth-grader)

```
Christmas
  Christ's Birthday
    Healer of people
      Died for our sins
        Savior.
```

(by a sixth-grader)

Variation B: first line contains two syllables which state the title;
second line contains four syllables describing the title; third line
contains six syllables expressing an action; fourth line has eight
syllables expressing a feeling; fifth line contains two syllables
which point back to the title. This is the more classic form of the
topic poem, and is called a cinquain.

```
Jesus
  Emmanuel
    Heals all of his people
      No greater love is possible
        Savior.
```

(from <u>Exchange, A Catechist Collection</u>,
Pflaum Publishing Co.)

★ 5.   Write free verse. (Don't worry about rhyme, meter, or sentence structure.)

<u>Christ In Our World Today</u>

Where is He today?
He is in our world today and everyday.
He is with us wherever we go--

in a package sent to a needy family in Appalachia,
in the man who risks his life for others,
in a hospital,
on a ship,

in the teenager giving of her time for another person,
in the doctor finding a cure for cancer,
in the friendship offered to the ignored,
in peace shared by black and white,

in love--<u>that</u> is Christ in our world--
Christ is in us--in man himself--and with us--and
    in our world.
Now--in 1970.

    (a poem by eighth-graders)

 6. Write new words for a song.

    Thank you, for all my friends and family
    Thank you, for every man alive
    Thank you, may everyone who's living join in thanking you.

    Thank you, for every bird and flower
    Thank you, for every starry sky
    Thank you, for all your strength and power we shall glorify.

    Thank you, for giving me tomorrow
    Thank you, for giving me the sun
    Thank you, for being here beside me, thanks from everyone.

    (sung to tune of "Thank You" from <u>Accent on Youth</u> album,
    Mercury Records)

 7. Complete a sentence or phrase. (The teacher writes the phrase on the board; each student finishes it.) Many students who do not write easily can be encouraged to write <u>one</u> good sentence at a time. The results can be discussed, lettered on an appropriate magazine picture or picket sign, or used on bulletin boards.

    "My picture of Christ is . . ."

    "If we kill our brother . . ."

    "I wonder . . ."

    "I believe . . ."

 8. Write personal reflections (it is better not to call it a "theme") on what has been presented in class, or events in school life, newspapers, and so forth.

    "Love is found in the most unexpected places. It is the quiet moments, when words are never needed to express one's feelings. It is like watching the great melodramatic sunset, knowing that, somehow, it is being staged only for you.

"It is the way you feel when you talk to someone, and they don't tell you to be quiet or to go away.

"Love comes quietly, when you are sad or lonely. All of a sudden it is there beside you, holding your hand and smiling up at you. Then, suddenly, you aren't lonely anymore.

"Love is always there when you want it. All you have to do is care."

Anne Mockley, Grade 8

"Love came forth to the world to make the grass greener, the sky bluer, the flowers brighter, the mountains smoother, people happier."

Suzanne Scherer, Grade 4

9. Write about a scriptural event as though you were an eyewitness writing it for a newspaper (or your diary or a TV script, or a letter to someone).

"Jeremiah called pacifist, jailed for leading anti-war demonstration . . ."

"Dear Mother and Dad,
Today Paul and I are stopping for the night just outside Corinth. We are camping in the open to avoid the inns. We are afraid that the police who ran us out of Thessalonika have sent word to have us arrested before we can join the Christians in Corinth."

10. Write an acrostic.

Take the word LEADER, and think of a quality that a good leader possesses, using words beginning with each of those letters. Then discuss the qualities each person thought of, and finally discuss these in terms of Jesus Christ as our leader.

Note: acrostics and crossword puzzles are essentially mechanical exercises. Unless they are used with care in the lesson they will be nothing more than a vocabulary test or a time-wasting gimmick.

Chapter 7: BOOKLETS

Workbooks or scrapbooks are useful for all age levels. They can combine:

> original stories or poems
> themes in response to thought questions
> pictures (crayon and magic markers are convenient,
>   but anything goes--torn paper, paint, etc.)
> information gathered by research.

A booklet is an excellent way of culminating a unit, initiating research, or deepening a concept. Use a looseleaf binder, or (for younger children) pages stapled together. Give it a lovely cover, display it (them), explain them to other classes, bring them to the altar in an offertory procession, show them to the pastor or parents, keep them as personal "catechisms" to look at later.

For ideas on various artistic techniques useful in making booklets, look through the "VISUAL ARTS" chapters.

For Instance:

  make a

  booklet . . .

. . . on the Mass, with pictures, explanations, outlines of the structure, copy of the Canon prayers, an original Canon, favorite hymns, original vestment designs.

. . . on the seasons of the Church year.

. . . of magazine pictures and newspaper articles illustrating a scriptural or doctrinal theme in modern life.

. . . of scriptural quotations; including drawings or comments.

. . . of a scriptural theme (sin and reconciliation, Exodus-Covenant, love of neighbor, prayer); include drawings of the biblical events which center on this theme, scriptural quotations (nicely lettered), magazine pictures illustrating this theme in modern life, relevance of the theme.

. . . of great Christian (religious) persons; choose from the biblical personages, saints, contemporary figures, persons they know, famous people.

. . . of notes on outside reading (congratulations, if your students do any!).

. . . a religious autobiography; mention sacraments received or other strong religious experiences (date, place, sponsors, officiating minister, significance of the event, drawing or photo of it), favorite scriptural passages or themes, personal reflections on being a Christian, views on life in the Church today, "why I am a Christian," photos of self, family, description of people who have influenced them.

. . . an illustrated Bible (best done as a cooperative project). For primary children, cut construction paper and writing paper to equal sizes. Ask the children to write in brief what they have learned on writing paper, and then illustrate it on the construction paper. Staple the papers and the illustrations together and add a cover. This project might take several weeks or months.

Chapter 8: THE VISUAL ARTS (Two Dimensions)

"MY OWN THING"

A blank sheet of paper and a paint
brush call for a unique personal
response. No one can ever paint
this picture again, it is mine, I did it. A child who puts really
personal, creative effort into portraying a religious theme on a
banner or mural is forced to think and feel for himself or herself
and interiorize the religious message. When the class has an open
accepting attitude toward art, the children are able to show others
(and discover for themselves) things they have learned, things that
have happened, things that are important to them.

   Art is one of the indispensable ways in which men and women share
in God's creativity. Through art we express and deepen our sensitivity toward beauty, and our awareness of reality. It can be used
to show graphically a story, a mood, a feeling, or a thought. Art
may "look like" something (representational, realistic) or it may
not (abstract).

   Not every drawing a child makes will be "good art," and no such
judgments are placed on a child's work. It is not the "artiness"
of the product that counts, but the student's involvement with the
project and with the reality being portrayed. However, the teacher
should help build the children's confidence and skill in expressing
themselves visually through the sensitive use of TEXTURE, COLOR,
LINE, and FORM. The children also, of course, learn from one another.

GENERAL PROCEDURES: see page 11--add the general
    recommendation that all necessary equipment be
    easily accessible to the children.

Projects can be given to an individual or committee.
    The entire class can work on one project if they
    are divided into committees with specific tasks.

Projects are as flexible as possible but not vague.

The time allotted should be in proportion to the value
    of the experience. It can be a few minutes for
    a crayon drawing to accompany an original poem, or
    a few months for a booklet, built up page by page.
    Painting elaborate backdrops for a dramatization
    is a waste of time since it is more mechanical
    than thought-provoking.

art is the work of a person

    a human being

  who is free to take into himself what he sees outside

    and from his free center

      put his human stamp on it

the artist is the sign to the whole world

    that reality

      or the world

    is shaped by man

      and not the other way around

— Corita

THE VISUAL ARTS: (Two Dimensions)

TABLE OF CONTENTS

Make a PAINTING

1. WITH PAINT

    Urge the children to draw with the paint brush directly, without using a pencil.

    People should be put in the picture first; then background.

    Remind them to draw large and fill the whole paper, using strong, bright colors.

    For the center of interest, the most important people or things should be larger and more colorful than the others.

 Capture the feeling of an especially happy event.
    After discussing the experience, talk about how colors show feelings. Each child completely covers a piece of paper with the color that best expresses the event for him or her. When it is completely dry, the child chooses either a tint or shade of that same color, and draws a picture in dry-brush technique. Keep the brush dry and the idea fresh.

 Paint parallel pictures.
    Paint a picture of Israelite slavery in Egypt and economic or racial "slavery" today; Abraham going into an unknown country and the astronauts going into unknown space.

 Paint a story.
    After reading and discussing The Gift of the Magi, a short story by O. Henry, students try to think of experiences in which they or someone else gave a gift that required real sacrifice. They then translate these remembered situations into "stories" told by means of four pictures that are painted on the sides of large grocery boxes. After showing their art and sharing their experiences with each other, these examples of sacrifice are stacked to be used as the base for a temporary altar (or arranged in front of the permanent altar). The children then share in the Eucharistic sacrifice, in this way finding a deeper meaning in their own experiences.

    For this activity a thick mixture of tempera should be used, with a little liquid detergent added to facilitate covering advertisements printed on the boxes. For best results completely cover the printing with a dark color; when dry, paint figures on this background with the lighter colors, using paint sparingly (i.e. avoiding puddles or drips) in quick strokes, and adding only the minimum of detail to tell the "story."

(From Exchange, a Catechist Collection, Pflaum Publishing Co.)

2. WITH PAPER

Have sheets and/or scraps of colored paper, glue, and scissors on hand. For variation let children tear the paper rather than cut it.

Cut or tear parts for the picture from construction paper, or use large colored pages from magazines, or wallpaper sample books, or colored tissue paper. Glue them to another piece of colored paper used as background.

Colored tissue paper gives some lovely effects when used for the entire picture, or mixed with the solid shapes torn from construction paper. Use Crystal Craft or a similar art tissue. A mixture of 1/2 Elmer's Glue and 1/2 water is painted over the entire surface of the shape or on the background paper. The shape is dropped carefully on the background (white background is best, as stiff a paper or cardboard as possible) because it cannot be moved without smearing the color. The tissue forms new colors when shapes overlap, creating interesting effects. After it is thoroughly dry, lettering can be added.

(This technique is best with intermediate and upper grades only.)

 Make a picture of the Little Prince's Flower.
    For a unit on friendship read the passages in The Little Prince by Antoine de St. Exupery which tell of his care and love for his flower. Let the children make a picture of the flower with bright paper (torn-paper technique and colored tissue would be very effective). A three-dimensional flower can be made by folding or crumpling the paper before gluing it down.

 Make a picture of the joy of the resurrection.
    Ask the children to portray the joy and glory of the resurrection (not just the standard empty-tomb picture) with brightly colored paper. These could be done in the shape of stained glass windows.

HELP THE CHILDREN PREPARE TO DRAW A SCENE BY STIMULATING
THEIR IMAGINATIONS BEFORE THEY BEGIN:

"Close your eyes. Visualize your picture. What people
are there? What are they doing? What are they wearing?
Where are they? What else is in the picture?"

3. WITH SCRAFFITO

Completely cover a sheet of heavy manila paper or drawing paper
with patches of bright colors using crayons and pressing heavily.
Color the entire sheet again heavily with black crayon, covering
all the bright colors. Black liquid tempera mixed with a little
liquid detergent will serve the same purpose. Allow the tempera
to dry thoroughly before proceeding to the next step.

Since this preparation of the scraffito paper is very time-
consuming, it can be done at home, then brought to class for
the final step.

With a large nail or scissor-edge or stick (anything that will
scratch off the black crayon or tempera), lightly scrape the
black surface until the color underneath shows through. The
wider the scraping tool, the wider the line of color. Scrape
out the desired scene or design, and the resulting picture has
a stained-glass effect.

 Make a set of pictures on the seasons.
        The colors chosen for the background would be typical of
the season being illustrated. The scene or symbol scratched
out would then reveal colors that help convey the message of
the picture. This can be done for the seasons of the solar
year or the seasons of the church year.

4. WITH CRAYON-RESIST

Figures in the picture are colored heavily with crayons, and
then a thin wash of water color or tempera is brushed over the
whole picture, thus filling in the uncolored areas, and giving
the crayoned areas a jewel-like quality.

The wash should be of a color that will contrast with or set
off the colors used with the wax crayons.

57

Make a picture symbolic of ministry.
      Plan the design on "the meaning of ministry today" on
scrap paper first. Be sure that the symbols are bold, different from the usual stereotyped ones, exaggerated, meaningful. Students could work in small groups, so that they can
come up with new designs through discussion.

5. WITH COLORED CHALK

      Wet the paper thoroughly, or use dry paper and dip the chalk in
water as it is used. This makes the chalk adhere to the paper
rather than the child! If chalk work is not done on wet paper,
spray it with an art fixitive or spray-net.

      Chalk is less satisfying on small individual pictures than it is
with murals. It is excellent for murals! It gives good bright
color effects. Be sure to buy chalk in bright artist's colors
at an art, office, or school supply house--not the pale collection
sold in most dime stores.

 Make a mural on baptism.
      Trace the water theme in Scripture, scene by scene: The
Spirit moved over the waters at creation, the Ark, the Red Sea,
the Jordan, and so on.

 Make a mural on creation.
      With colored chalk the teacher draws a rough outline of
the profile of the earth on the chalkboard or a large sheet of
butcher or billboard paper. It should not be portrayed as a
smooth circle, but rather some hills or mountains should be
included, as well as a large sea and some valley or flat land.
This sketch should be drawn large enough to allow the children
space for adding more details, with many children working at
once on the chalk drawing. This activity would follow a lesson on the wonder of creation and focus the students' attention
on the use we have made of the created universe.
      The teacher begins, "How do people use the sea and the
ocean?" As the children offer answers, they receive pieces of
colored chalk and draw a quick sketch of people using water in
the way they suggested (e.g., a person swimming, some fishermen). Continue: "For what do we use land? mountains? smaller
lakes or streams? tall trees? other plants? What do we find
under the soil that we use?"* As each child comes up with a
concrete answer, he or she draws that activity.
      The teacher keeps the conversation going, with four or five
children drawing at once, and makes sure that all children have
an opportunity to add to the mural.

*(From Life, Love, Joy grade 3 teacher's manual, by Janaan Manter-
   nach and Carl Pfeifer, revised by Elizabeth Jeep, Silver Burdett,
   1974.)

6. **WITH CRAYON AND SANDPAPER**

A delightful "one-time" technique for young children (6 to 8).
The effect is vibrant, and especially good for happy themes.

Make a MOSAIC

The wooden ends of an orange crate or other scrap wood can be used as the
base. Break colored glass bottles, old vases, figurines, and so forth by
holding them between two thick pads of newspaper and crushing them with a
hammer.

Create a design by gluing the glass chips to the board. Elmer's and
Sobo and airplane glue are good. If the board is covered with the design,
and the pieces are fitted together, grout may be used (but is not necessary). If the size of the glass pieces is varied, an added textural effect
is achieved. If the board is not covered, the open areas can be painted
or varnished.

Besides broken glass, try pebbles, tile, or crushed and dyed eggshell. (For the eggshell technique, wash, dry, drop shells in water dyed with food coloring or other dye, remove, dry, crush. Draw on the background with glue--use directly from dispenser bottle. Sprinkle eggshell on wet glue, pat gently to embed it in glue, shake off excess.)

 Make a crucifix.

 Make a wall plaque with the Hebrew name for God.

(This medium lends itself well to symbol, and is best with older children --10 to 14.)

Make a MURAL

A mural is just an extended picture or series of pictures.

Paint, colored paper, colored chalk, or magazines (collage technique) make the best murals. Crayon is not bright enough to be satisfying.

Large sheets of paper are needed. For best results the work space should not be cramped. The paper can be spread out on the floor (move the desks or use the hall) or a cafeteria table or playground.

See page 58 for more ideas on colored chalk.

 Make a mural (or time line) of salvation history.
Plan with the children the scenes which will be portrayed and who will work on each scene. Some children could write out the story of each event and glue it to the mural. This is a useful approach for any chronological theme, such as Old Testament, life of Christ, and so on.

 Make a mural of "the Christian in action."
Instead of separate scenes, help the children design a unified city landscape which includes people acting with Christian love in various buildings (home, hospital, school, business, store, etc.) and various situations (an accident, shopping, studying, etc.).

Make a mural emphasizing God's love for each person.

Each child paints a self-portrait and his or her name on the mural paper. In the center of the mural someone paints the words, "God loves me." (This is especially good for young children.) For best results let the children take turns at the mural, two or three at a time, while the rest of the class proceeds with other activities.

 Make a mural on the sacraments.

Show a person growing from infancy to old age, participating in the sacramental life of the Church, from baptism to annointing of the sick. The scenes can be continuous, one phase running into another.

 Make a mural of helping hands (or following feet).

Each child makes handprints on the paper with tempera paint or water-soluble ink (just pour paint into a pie tin that has a sponge in it). Someone adds the words "Here are the hands to do the work of Christ" or "Did you not know that I must be about my Father's business?" or "Into your hands I commend my Spirit."

Or trace the hands in different positions. Show the hands of a teacher, mother, minister, foreman.

Or make a mural of footprints, with the words "Come, follow me" or something else that is appropriate.

 Make a mural on unity.

Cut paper shapes of churches, temples, synagogues, and shrines. Sponge tempera paint around shapes so that the open spaces are covered. Remove paper shapes, fill in details of buildings with yarn.

Make a GIANT "FILMSTRIP"*

Decide on the story line, write the narration, and create the pictures which tell the story. This is best done by a committee of three to six children. The pictures can be made with crayon, paint, felt tip pens, or colored paper, but should be large and bright enough to be seen by all the class. The pictures could also be done with spatter-paint technique. Cut out silhouettes of the figures in the story, place them on a piece of paper, creating one scene. Use spray paint or the old wire screen (or finger) and toothbrush routine with tempera. Then the silhouettes can be reused in other scenes.

The children can present their "filmstrip" to the class by holding up the pictures one by one as someone reads (or ad-libs) the narration. The room can be darkened and a flashlight shone on the pictures.

 Make a filmstrip of two children who quarrel and are later reconciled.

 Make a filmstrip of the ceremonies of the Easter vigil.

Make a COLLAGE (Montage, Assemblage)

A collage is a paste-up of things that are somehow different--pieces of paper that have different designs, pieces of cloth that have different textures, or a combination of different things such as cloth, paper, weeds, buttons, and an old belt buckle. These objects, on the other hand, do have something in common, and the final collection of things makes a total statement of some kind. Collages of magazine photos and ads are especially popular, and additional ideas regarding them are contained in a later section of this chapter, "Think about MAGAZINES."

Large collages can be created in a single class session if the teacher is well prepared. A large class can be divided into working groups so that every member is able to make a significant contribution. Time limits should be set or children will invariably stretch this activity into several sessions.

*(For information on making genuine filmstrips see Chapter 10.)

Everyone can work on the collage simultaneously or the teacher can cut one or more large sheets of poster board into sections, being careful to mark the top of each section so that they can be reassembled later without having to turn the children's work upside down. If the shape is irregular the teacher can use an arrow similar to the marking for the "straight of the fabric" on a dress pattern.

After the theme of the activity has been discussed, each student or small committee will then receive one section, and cover it with drawings, photos, magazine pictures and/or found objects (ticket stubs, letters, leaves, shoe laces, cabbages and kings!). This work can be done in class or at home. When all is complete, the individual sections are presented, examined and discussed, then assembled into a single large production (or several if the class is especially large). This can be accomplished by holding the edges of the pieces together with masking tape on the back, or by mounting them on a larger piece of contrasting paper--letting a margin of the paper show between them.

Many interesting shapes and designs can be made with the collage. Small rectangular or square sections can, of course, be assembled in a rectangle, quilt-fashion, or the sections can be pie-shaped or triangular, and then assembled to form a starburst, a flower or a three-dimensional pyramid. Petal or teardrop sections can be assembled in a number of patterns, such as a flower. The center of the flower can be a circle with a word or quotation pertinent to the theme, or with patches of bright tissue paper.

Make a unity collage.
    At the end of a session on "In the Important Things We are All One," the class should list all the needs that people have in common. The list is then reduced to categories (e.g., the need to work) and the children are asked to bring in all the pictures they can find relating to any of the categories (e.g., mowing the lawn). At the next class period the pictures are quickly separated and a committee assigned to make a collage of each "need," with the appropriate pictures, some glue, and a triangular piece of poster board. Finally all the "needs" are mounted together in an attractive pattern on a large piece of paper, an explanatory caption is painted on, and it is hung in the school or church hall for others to enjoy.

(From "Exchange," The Catechist, January 1973.)

Make a reconciliation collage.

    Each student receives a jig-saw puzzle shaped piece of paper (with the "front, top" marked) to make into a name tag. After the lesson (on "break-up/make-up" or "working together" or some other aspect of community), the students are asked to fit their tags (representing themselves, their talent, contribution, creativity, insight) together so

that the result is a close-fitting whole. As students find a fit they
tape the tags together until the whole puzzle is complete. (Symboliz-
ing the fact that the class is incomplete when anyone "holds back" his
gifts or his participation.) It is important for the teacher to join
in this activity. This activity is especially meaningful in the early
part of the year.

Make a friendship collage.

A person's friends have personalities that are quite different
from his or her own, but they can achieve great harmony and friendship.
Show that many things which we never think of putting together can form
a very harmonious collage.

To a large piece of construction paper glue an interesting design
cut from newspaper. It should be large enough almost to fill the paper. Next use different media to make the picture more interesting.
For example, cut a design on the flat side of a halved potato; use it
as a rubber stamp, printing the design in various colors. Add buttons,
popsicle sticks, and whatever else will make the finished piece surprising and pleasing to the eye.

Make a TODAY collage.

Use magazines, newspapers, objects, which, when put together, will
offer a commentary on modern life.

Think about COLOR

Show how colors mix.

For a lesson on how people mix together to form a community which
is more than just the sum of its parts, show the children how blue and
yellow paint (or food coloring in water, or colored tissue) will become
a whole new color (green) when mixed together. Red and yellow make
orange, and red and blue make purple. But yellow and blue is the most
startling.

This is suitable only for very young children. This activity could
be followed by a reading of Little Blue and Little Yellow by Leo Lionni.

Show how colors harmonize.

The children can study the harmony in creation by seeing how well
all the colors go together. The teacher can spread various kinds of
colored paper out and ask the children to see if they can find three
colors that are ugly and that do not look pleasing together. (It is
virtually impossible!)

Study the FEELING of Lent.

Which colors would you use to show the feelings of Lent, sorrow, hurt, sadness, suffering, repentence? Is the Church's traditional use of purple suitable? Which colors express the feelings of Easter--joy, newness, glory, resurrection? Make a mosaic of torn-paper shapes showing the transition from Lent to Easter, from death to life, from winter to spring.

 Visualize a musical composition.

Do this by interpreting the music (an instrumental record is best) in color and line and form. Try Handel's Messiah, or the Grand Canyon Suite.

Think about LINE and SHAPE

Some shapes give a feeling of stability (circle, fat triangle) while others give a feeling of nervousness (jagged edges) or stiffness (a thin straight line). Some of the feelings usually ascribed to lines and shapes are:

circle: happiness, unity, fullness
triangle: conflict, disunity, stability
straight line: rigidity, coldness, directness
jagged line: turmoil, conflict, tension

When the children perceive meanings in shapes and lines different from those commonly understood, they should not be told it is wrong. Each person has past connections or associations with colors and shapes that give him special meanings. For instance, a little girl may think that a zig-zag is the most beautiful line in the whole world because of a favorite dress which has a border of that design.

 Tell a story with shapes.

How did Adam and Eve feel when they said "No" (disobeyed)? How do we feel when we say "No"? What kind of shape looks like that feeling? What kind of line? What shapes look like "Yes"? Make a "No" design and a "Yes" design. Choose appropriate colors.

 Show the two possibilities in life.

On one side of a piece of paper make a design of shapes and lines showing tranquility, unity, and peace. On the other show disunity and conflict.

> An artist is not a special kind of person.
> Every person is a special kind of artist.
> St. Thomas Aquinas

65

Think about SYMBOL

"It is only with the heart that one can see rightly;
what is essential is invisible to the eye." St. Exupery

Since so much of religious education deals with the essential, it is not
surprising that there is an emphasis on symbol in catechetics today. A
symbol is something that represents more than merely itself.

Children should be made familiar with traditional Christian symbols
(water, bread, cross, vestments) which have a sacramental role of helping
us to understand, communicate with, and relate to God. They should also
be helped to discover new symbols in their world.

 Study the "Sacred Place" symbol.
   The presence and accessibility of God has always been symbolized by
a place in the community set aside as God's dwelling. Have groups or
individual students write reports on the sacred places of various religious groups. Discuss the benefit and the danger of this symbol.

 Study the use of the cross in the history of the Christian Church.
   Make cross medallions of plaster of paris as the culmination of
the lesson. Use a variety of shapes and decorations. Pour the plaster onto waxed paper, shape it with fingers, stick a paper clip into
it before it dries, thread yarn through it to hang it around your
neck. Draw finishing touches with tempera, felt tip marker, or India
ink.

 Make symbols of the resurrection.
   Ask the children to list the traditional symbols for Easter and
the resurrection (empty tomb, lily, jeweled cross). Then ask them
to think of new ones, and make a set of posters portraying them.
They will think of such things as butterflies coming from the cocoon,
chicks hatching from the shell, sunrise, new leaves on the "dead"
branch, and so on.

 Make name tags.
   My name is a symbol to me. In a lesson on the uniqueness of each
person, let the children make name tags for themselves (or signs for
their desks), decorating the card with their favorite colors, their
favorite things, and so on.

Make a name design.

Fold a piece of paper in half, lengthwise. Open it up and write your name on one half with dark crayon, using the fold as a line. Close the paper again and rub it. When it is opened again the crayon will have left a mirror image on the other half of the paper. Trace over all lines with crayons, decorate as a design.

Make a BULLETIN BOARD

Bulletin boards are one of the most flexible tools for visualizing and displaying things in the classroom. They can employ all the artistic and creative contributions of teacher and students. The best boards follow the rules of commercial art: simplicity (ONE idea at a time), variety, and focus (emphasize the center of interest as you would in a picture).

Allow the children to plan and execute the bulletin-board displays as part of the lesson itself.

CREATE IMAGINATIVE BULLETIN BOARDS!

Make a resolution to help someone.

The bulletin board is covered with dark paper. Another piece of paper, the same size, is torn (artistically!) into as many pieces as there are people in the class, including teacher and helpers. Since you will want to fit the pieces together again later, be sure that everyone can tell the back from the front.

Each child traces his or her hand on the front side of the piece-- and writes a resolution (in pencil) around it. It is taken home as a reminder. When the resolution to help someone has been carried out, the child brings back the paper, draws a picture inside the hand of what was done and pins it to the bulletin board in its original place. The resolution was written in pencil so that it can be changed if any of the children were unrealistic in their choices. When all the children have finished, all the pieces of the jig-saw puzzle will be back in place.

 Make a bulletin board on "unity".

Each child draws or paints figures of any kind of person (doctor, mail carrier, automechanic, parent) about six inches tall. They are cut out and pinned to the board in the shape of a human body. A child draws a large head of Christ, proportionate to the body thus formed, and it is added. After discussing the unity of all persons in Christ, the students now add the words "We, though many, are one body, all of us who join in the one bread," which point to the signi- ficance of the Eucharist as the effective sign of Christian unity.

Make a BANNER

A banner is usually a striking and dynamic proclamation of a message through picture, design, or word. Any theme, phase of the Church year, celebration, event, or insight can be the subject of a banner. Religious poetry, psalms, prophetic statements, parts of the liturgy, famous quotations, original prayers, or contemporary literature can be a source of inspiration.

A religious banner is usually hung in the church or place of celebra- tion. It can be placed behind the altar, on the side wall, or in the ves- tibule. It can be mounted on poles and placed in flag-stands (or sand- filled waste-baskets camouflaged with bright paper), or hung on the wall, or carried in procession, or given to a friend, or all of those things! They can be used to brighten the home or religious education building. A mini-banner can be mailed to a friend.

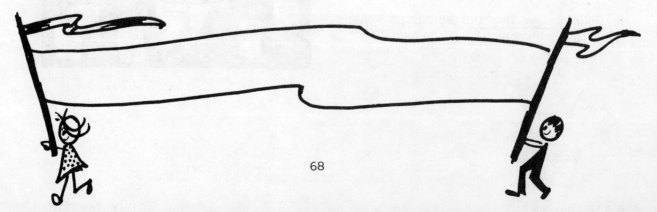

GENERAL PROCEDURES:

1. Choose a topic.

2. Choose a shape and size.
    (Have the courage to do a really large banner
    sometime!)

3. Choose a background.
    Cloth: corduroy, burlap, linen, cotton, muslin,
    an old sheet, upholstery or drapery mater-
    ial.
    Paper: long sheets of newsprint, butcher paper,
    wrapping paper--white or brown--adver-
    tising paper, poster paper, tagboard.

    A bright print or stripe often makes an excel-
    lent banner, whether in cloth or paper. Words
    can be added with felt, paint, or magic marker.

4. Plan the design, draw it on scrap paper.
    Details of the design can change if necessary as
    the banner is being made.

    Either lettering or a figure should dominate the
    design, or the banner will become too "busy" and
    confusing. For a banner on which lettering alone
    will be used it is sometimes good to give the
    paper some interest--blow paint splotches across
    it, give it a strong splash of a weak color or
    a contrasting color, give it some sprinkles of
    a strong color. Allow this to dry before the
    lettering is added.

    The message, colors, styles of lettering used,
    and the design itself should work together to
    create a mood.

    A teacher who is aware of the basic principles
    of design is able to give the children a great
    deal of insight into planning successful banners.

5. Execute the design.
    Be sure that TIME, SPACE, MATERIALS, and DESIGN are all organ-
    ized before beginning the banner!

    Cut fabric or paper to correct size. Paint, paste, color, and
    so on.

Use: tempera (extra thick for cloth), felt tip markers, India
      ink, textile paint (for a permanent fabric banner),

      felt, fabric scraps (use only one kind or mix colors and
      textures),

      yarn, embroidery thread, ric-rac,

      buttons, beads, etc.

Glue or sew yarn or fabric pieces to a fabric
      banner for permanence. Pin or baste
      letters to a background cloth which
      will be used again.
Utilize contrasts in color and texture.

THINK BIG!

 Have a banner procession.
      As a culminating event for vacation school, Palm Sunday, or other
religious day, help the children plan a celebration including banners.
The students can begin on the first day of vacation school to make
banners which illustrate what they are studying, or they begin several
weeks before Palm Sunday to discuss the meaning of Christ's triumphal
recognition in Jerusalem. All classes can participate on their own
level. Each child in the primary grades can make small (9 x 12) signs
or pennants to carry, while the upper grades can make group banners
of a more permanent type. The procession begins in the education
building, goes outside, and then into church for a liturgical service.

70

Make a SCROLL

For a wall-hanging-style scroll follow the same procedures as for banners--
add rods to top and bottom, hang with a piece of yarn. For a hand scroll,
such as those used in Jewish services, the rods are held in each hand, the
scroll viewed horizontally. If you are simulating the Hebrew scrolls it
can be composed so as to be read from right to left.

 This is my life.
    A hand-held scroll can be made showing the chief events in the
child's life, including hopes for the future. Use dowel rods, long
strip of paper, ribbon ties, paint or felt tip marker, or crayon.

                    Always there remains this need to explain
            to each other that we are good. We all have a constant need
                    to be reaffirmed.
        The single man needs this. The whole human race needs a yea--
            needs the large ceremonial pat on the back that says

                Come on, come on!
                We can make it!

                                            Corita

Think about GIFTS, CARDS & DECORATIONS

 Make a Christmas Card.
Make an envelope for it from bright wallpaper.

 Make a greeting card for an elderly person in the parish.
Decorate it with origami (folded paper) trees or birds or
other motif to give it three dimensions.

★ Make name tags for the friends in your neighborhood.

★ Make some pretty placemats and napkins for a celebration.
Weave paper strips together, or decorate a large piece
of construction paper with felt, yarn, crayon, and so
forth. Decorate the napkins with crayon, magic-marker.

For ideas on making your cards and decorations a little unusual, consult
your library for books on the arts of origami, cut paper and paper sculpture.

Think about LETTERING

Any number of methods can be used for communicating a written
message effectively and artistically, whether it is to be
done on a picture, poster, scroll, collage, banner, Christmas
card, vestment, or mural. Letters may be torn from paper,
cut from fabric, drawn and/or painted. Words can be spelled
out with letters cut from headlines or magazine advertisements. Lettering can be done with pencil, charcoal, pen,
brush, rubber stamps--using ink, paint, crayon (less satisfactory), felt tip markers, or a combination of these.

ABCDEFGHI JKLMNOP

If a variety of rubber type from the old flash card printing sets is available, an interesting and contemporary style can be achieved by mixing the sizes, caps, and lowercase letters to form a pleasing design. If this is not available, pink or green pearl erasers can be made into rubber stamps. When you are carving, however, remember to reverse the letters so they will not print a backward image.

SAY SI, SI

To convey a message effectively, be conscious of: sizes and shapes of the letters, uniformity of height and slant, and value contrast between letters and background. The words must become UNITS--the letters in each word should be close together, and the words themselves, farther apart.

grace Joy

HOPE

New

LOVE

A freedom in lettering is now in vogue which should prove a great advantage to teachers and students. No longer does the student have to strive to do the nearly impossible task of having every letter a perfect size and shape. It is important that the teacher understand this in directing the children. Lettering need not follow a straight line.

The children should be made aware of the fact that texture, shape, slant, or color can suggest the meaning of a word. Size of the letters can be varied so as to emphasize important words.

QRS
TUV
WXYZ

abc
de
fg
hi jklmnopgrstuvwxyz

Think about MAGAZINES

 Make a magazine candid* on "The World at Worship."

A unit on ecumenism can include a study of various modes of religious worship. The children can collect pictures during the course of the unit. National Geographic would probably be helpful here. The teacher or student could simply explain each picture as it was shown, without writing out a formal script. The presentation could include pictures of African tribes, ancient Druids at Stonehenge, American Indians, Aztex or Inca religious rituals, Greek and Roman temples, as well as modern Christian and non-Christian worship. Comparison with "pagan" religious practices would emphasize the basic unity of the Christian traditions.

*Directions for making a magazine candid are given in Chapter 16.

 Make a magazine candid expressing the idea that man has been redeemed
(yet he is still in need of redemption).

 Make a magazine candid on Christian repentence and reconciliation
(taking the parable of the Prodigal Son as the starting point).

 Make a magazine montage (pictures only) on work.
We are a corporate people--we depend upon and help each other. Make
a montage of people at work. Try to make it as varied as possible.

 Make a magazine collage of the Church.
Show that the Church is not a building, but people. Cut out magazine photos of people, glue them close together on a piece of advertising paper in the shape of a church. Letter "We, though many, are one
body" on the collage, or spell it out with letters cut from the magazine ads.

 Make a magazine mural on death and resurrection.
During Lent read the story of The Red Balloon by A. Lamorisse to the
class. Do not read the whole story, only up to the part where the boy's
balloon is crushed. How did the boy feel? Talk about how people feel
when they are lonely, made fun of, out of a job, sick. Let the children
draw a large picture of the boy and his balloon. Cut out a sad face for
the boy, and fill the balloon with pictures of suffering people.

After Easter, finish the story, talk about resurrection, how Christians restore life to people. Have a celebration, blow up some red
balloons, and so on.

 Make a booklet of magazine pictures on "I Am Alive."

It is a tremendous gift just to have been born into a world filled with possibilities. Select pictures that say "I am happy to be alive." The pictures are trimmed to the same size (5" x 10" is a good size), folded in half, and glued back to back in a staggered progression. When finished, both sides will be covered with pictures, and the book will open out like an accordion. Some suitable words can be included too, as well as a title page.

 Make a booklet on sin and mercy.

If the accordion type of booklet is used, one side can be sin, the other side mercy (joy, love, care, concern).

 THOSE WERE THE GOOD OLD DAYS !!!   ! !

Teaching religion "involves only three simple steps:

1) See the lesson in the text used by the pupil.
2) Note the suggestions given for teaching that lesson as found in the manual.
3) Teach the lesson accordingly.

(From Teacher's Manual for "Jesus And I," written in 1936.)

Chapter 9: THE VISUAL ARTS (Three Dimensions)

The use of the third dimension lends variety, and sometimes a deeper sense of reality to children's work. Folding, twisting, modeling, building, making, arranging, are very satisfying to all normal children, and can be of great value if used correctly and creatively in the religion program.

   A 3-D activity can be a large or a small project. It can take three minutes (finding a vase and clearing a space on the shelf for a flower), or it can take three weeks (building an altar). It can involve the use of a single medium (decorating an Easter egg with colors suggesting the joy and new life of the resurrection) or it can be complex (preparing the table for a Passover meal). Children can work alone, they can work in small groups, or all can work on one project.

   The scrap box will come in handy in most 3-D projects.

THE VISUAL ARTS: (THREE DIMENSIONS)

TABLE OF CONTENTS

NOTICE THINGS (found objects)

What is the value of learning that God created a beautiful world, once, billions of years ago--if we do not realize that we live in that world, and that we can watch His continuing work of creation going on all around us? Young children are open to this kind of learning, but need the stimulation of an adult who loves nature and can become excited about the beauty which can be found in the simplest objects. Rocks and leaves and flowers have texture, color, shape, pattern, size--we can help children to "see" these things for the first time. This is especially appropriate at the beginning of a new season, at Thanksgiving, and at Easter.

Make a nature plaque.
    Take a nature walk. Collect lovely pebbles, leaves, nuts. Pour enough plaster of paris to make a plaque on a scrap piece of plywood, or on a piece of cardboard or waxed paper. Arrange the objects collected on the walk in the wet plaster. Also put a wire loop (hairpin or paperclip) in it so that it can be hung when dry. The plaster will stick to the plywood or cardboard, giving it a "frame." It will not stick to the waxed paper.

    (Plaster of paris is quick, easy, and satisfying for young children to use, but they should be cautioned to keep from touching it while it is wet. If possible, allow things to dry overnight before the children take them home.)

Make a tree of life (an Easter tree).
    Start with a branch, add decorated eggs ("blow" the eggs so that they will be lightweight) and flowers.

Decorate Easter eggs.
    Instead of the standard procedure, try fine-tip magic-markers, yarn, lace, colored tissue scraps, and so forth. (Use Elmer's, Sobo, or airplane glue.)

Make a leaf window.
    Collect lovely leaves, grass, weeds. Arrange them on a sheet of waxed paper. Arrange scraps of tissue (colors appropriate to the season) and/or shavings of wax crayons on the paper too. Cover the whole thing with another sheet of waxed paper. Seal it with a warm iron (warm enough to melt wax and crayon shavings). Attach to a window so that the light shines through. Put construction paper (or something) around the edges for a "finished," "framed" look.

<u>Plant some seeds</u>.
     Talk about new life, waiting, dependence upon others (sun, water,
dirt), Easter, and so forth.

BUILD THINGS (construction)

Construction is the opposite of sculpture. In sculpture the artist chips
or scrapes away at the clay or stone, and arrives at the desired shape.
In construction the artist builds up to the final design by adding smaller
components to one another.

 <u>Build a communications wall</u>.
     What prevents people from talking to each other? from saying deep
things that they really feel? what are the barriers between individuals,
groups, nations?

     With large grocery cartons build a wall. Decorate it with paint,
magazine pictures, newspaper headlines, that show the barriers to communication.

     What helps people communicate? What brings men together? Make a
door or gateway on your wall and decorate it with these things.

     Instead of a wall, the children could build the "Tower of Babel"
using this technique.

 <u>Build a Scripture tower</u>.
     Tear pages from a magazine and roll them up like a pencil. They can
be used as they are, or can be painted. (Add some liquid detergent to
the paint so that it will stick to the slick paper.) Tape or glue it
so that it doesn't unroll. You will need from 50 to 500! Build a
skeleton-like tower by taping or stapling them together. In the open
spaces suspend three-dimensional objects (paper-sculpture, pipe cleaner,
<u>papier-mache</u>), symbolic of people or events in salvation history. Hang
the most ancient at the bottom so that when the tower is completed it
represents a time chart, culminating at the top with a symbol for Christ.

     Discuss with the children the way each period in history builds upon
the last--there is a continuity and progress in the relationship of God
and man.

     Sticks, dowels, or straws can be used instead of magazine rolls.

Make models of the "family."

Have primary children make figures of their families; discuss "family" and put figures in a little house. Then put figures in a church and discuss "the parish family," then put them in a downtown area and discuss the "one great family of God."

 Build the kingdom.

Children draw slips of paper from a hat, and make a model of whatever is on the paper. Make people 6" high, and other things in proportion to the people. On the paper is written King, Bride, Groom, Waiter, Table, Food, Wine, Priest (or Minister), Altar Boy (or Usher), Lector, Altar, Chalice, Bread, and Person ("person" is repeated enough times so that every child in the room except three have an assignment). Those three are told to make the banquet hall. Since the children do not know what figures are being made, or how they will fit together, anticipation builds up.

When all are finished, put the banquet hall where all can see, then read the parable of the King's Wedding Banquet, allowing the children to add their figures to the scene as appropriate. Then discuss the meaning of the parable. Who are the guests? Who is the groom? the king? the bride? What is the banquet? Replace the waiters with the altar boys and lector, replace the table with the altar, the food and wine with the bread and chalice. Remove king, bride, and groom (in what way are they present?). Add priest. Discuss.

A WORD ABOUT FIGURES

Children like to make symbolic objects, and animals, but they generally like to do human figures most of all. These can be made of pipe cleaners, with or without paper clothes. They can stand on a styrofoam or cardboard base. The figure can be made entirely of paper; a clothespin (not the clip kind) can be used--paint a face and give it cloth or paper clothes; papier-mache can be used by older children.

SHAPE THINGS (sculpture)

1. <u>PAPER SCULPTURE</u>

Give a piece of paper three dimensions by cutting, folding, pinning, pleating, twisting, curling, pasting, adding other colors--until it can stand alone, or hang gracefully by a thread, or decorate a bulletin board. When figures are given volume, a bulletin board can become twice as interesting. A spring of accordion-pleated paper keeps pieces rounded out.

Paper folding (Origami) can be used in religion (for example, paper birds for lessons on nature, creation, etc.), but can be so absorbing that it distracts attention from the lesson taught.

 <u>Make paper flowers.</u>
Give them to the old person who lives in your neighborhood!

 <u>Illustrate Psalm 135.</u>
Then hang the paper figures on a mobile, stand in a circle around it, and sing Father River's "Bless the Lord." Tell the children in advance that their paper sculptures will be hung--a figure is balanced differently if it hangs rather than stands up.

2. <u>WIRE SCULPTURE</u>

Wire stimulates a high level of creativity since students seldom have stereotyped concepts for this medium. Any kind of wire may be used. Use pliers to bend strong wire. It is more satisfying, however, to bend it with one's hands--especially for younger children. The approach to animals, figures, or abstract construction varies with the material. One might start with a piece of soft stove wire about 4 feet in length, bending it in the middle to shape a head, then following the contour down to the shoulders, arms, body, legs, feet, and back up the other side. The approach is the same for either human figure or animal, standing on two feet or four. This body might be strengthened by taking additional wire and weaving it up and down the arms and legs and around the body as one visualizes the structure of the muscles and body tendons. Coiling it around parts of the body gives an entirely different effect.

Using the contour wire figure as a base, the student can thicken the figure by squeezing bulky scraps into the body parts and then wrapping with light wire. Another approach is to create an open skeleton by giving the body bulk with circular or looped wires attached to the basic figure. These are usually spaced an inch or so apart and go around both the width and the length of the body.

Abstracts can get off to a good start with coat-hanger wire bent into strong directional shapes. The use of lighter wires can be used to create

positive and negative relationships as well as **linear movements**. With
this type of work the rhythmic repetition of wire lines is important.

Children often try to work with too small figures, creating those
that lack character and a feeling of design. Some try working too large
and must make several starts before getting the basic contour down to
the proper size. They visualize the sculpture as a silhouette and must
be reminded to add bulk. Remind them to look at it from all directions
as they build it.

 Make a wire sculpture.
One that expresses the joy and glorious "feeling" or resurrection;
perhaps colored cellophane can be glued to some planes made by the
wire.

 With one continuous piece of wire.
Show Mary and Martha.

3. SAND CASTING

Sand casting is an exciting sculpture project that can be done in the
classroom as well as on the beach. The first step is to dampen an adequate supply of sand, in a sturdy box or carton.

The child decides on a subject, then draws its outline in the damp
sand with finger or stick. The sand on the inside of the outline is
scooped out with a tablespoon, to a depth of 2 or 3 inches.

If any decoration is to be added to the piece, now is the time to
do it. For an example, if the butterfly wings would look nice with
small pieces of colored glass, or if the fish is to have blue scales
of ceramic fragments, press these pieces face down very lightly in the
sand, in the area where you wish them to show up in the final product.

Next pour plaster of paris or hot wax into the sand "mold," allow
to dry, then remove your finished work.

 Make a crucifix.
Use bright chips of colored glass or pebbles, to give the shape of
of Jesus.

 Cast figures for a baptism mobile.
Let the children decide what best symbolizes the meaning and rite
of that important sacrament.

4. CLAY MODELING

Modeling can be done with clay, plasticine, papier-mache, or dough.
Water base clay is messier, but more exciting and satisfying for chil-

dren to work with than plasticine. It dries and can be painted or
fired in a kiln. Clay is an earth material and results are more dynamic when the earth qualities of sturdiness, strength, and bulk are
preserved.

When the classroom situation prohibits use of earth clay, the best
substitute is home-made play-dough. It is non-toxic, inexpensive,
easy to make and a delight to young children. If kept moist and pliable
in a plastic container it can be used over and over. It can also be
allowed to harden so that the children can take their figures home,
but it will be brittle and delicate, and cannot be fired.

        Recipe for play-dough: 2 cups flour
                                 1 cup salt
                                 2 cups water
                                 2 tablespoons oil
                                 3 to 4 teaspoons cream of tartar

                                 Cook and stir until it is of cookie dough
                                 consistency. Cool and knead. Add food
                                 coloring if desired. Cover tightly.

 Make a creche.

 Make a holder for your Easter candle.
    Do not give directions for a specific shape, but allow each child
to model a holder to his or her liking. Do this after their candles
are made so that it will be a good fit.

5. PAPIER-MACHE

Tear strips of newspaper, dip in wheat paste or diluted polymer medium
or diluted Elmer's Glue (wheat paste is cheaper, polymer and glue
stronger, quicker drying, and waterproof). Wrap the strip aroung a
basic form made from dry newspaper wads, cut cardboard, a dish, a tin
can, a clay model, or a balloon. Add the moistened strips layer upon
layer until everything hangs together and has the desired shape. The
figure can be painted a solid color while wet, details added when dry.
It can be decorated with torn pieces of colored tissue (put on with
Elmer's or polymer), yarn, and so forth.

A more authentic though messier process involves soaking newspaper
strips until they become pulp (overnight should do it) and then using
the pulp like modeling clay. The objects thus formed require more
time for drying than those made with the strip method. An "instant"
form of papier-mache is now available at hobby and art stores. It is
useful for small projects.

Prepare a seder table.
    Make the goblet, seder plate, and menorah. Even the special foods
(bitter herbs, lamb bone, egg, Matzoh, parsley, and haroseth) can be
made of papier-mache.

 Make life symbols.
    The children can discuss the various communities to which they belong
(family, school, class, congregation); activities they are engaged in,
things that are important to them, etc. All of these things can be
symbolized somehow, and that symbol made in papier-mache. The symbols
can be hung on a giant mobile, brought to the altar in an offertory
procession, and so forth.

HANG THINGS (mobiles)

A mobile is a group of two- or three-dimensional figures hung so that they
swing freely in the air. They can be made by an individual, but it is
easier to work out the balance if several people are working on it. It
may be wise to ask the children to include at least three objects (an odd
number is usually more artistic.)

    A coat hanger forms a simple base. It may be helpful for very young
children, who can hang four or five objects from it without having to worry
about balance. The objects will twirl on their strings, but they will not
interact with each other--hence it is not, properly speaking, a mobile.
This is not as attractive or satisfactory as a genuine mobile.

    Older children, who can cope with counterweight problems, can design
more satisfactory mobiles with thread (string, yarn) and rods (sticks,
dowels, cross piece cut from a coat hanger). Three rods are usually sufficient for beginners to achieve a successful mobile. Hang the rods close
enough to objects to give unity, but far enough apart so that nothing
touches as it swings. It is a good idea to sketch the mobile before hang-
ing it.

 Make a mobile on King David.
    Hang items symbolic of his life, reign, connection with Christ, con-
temporary relevance.

 Make a "Swimmy" mobile.
    Read the book Swimmy by Leo Lionni (Pantheon). Discuss the Christian
implications of the theme (Swimmy is a savior, the red fish must work
together, they can symbolize the Church, etc.). Compare to the fish
theme in the New Testament (fishers of men, kingdom is a net thrown
into the sea, etc.) and early Church (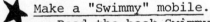 is sign of Christ or
the Christian).

84

Make a "My Time" mobile.

Each child draws a clock face on a paper plate. Then pictures of personal activities performed at each hour of a normal day are drawn. They need not do 24--one for school, one for sleeping, and so forth will do. These pictures can be drawn on small cards, or backed with cardboard and then cut out. The paper plate is hung face down, the pictures hung from the appropriate time on the clock face (for example, hang the "eating lunch" picture from the 12). Discussion can center around the amount of time spent with other people, the kinds of activities we are engaged in when we are with other people, and so on.

 Make an Easter mobile

or Christmas, or Lent, or Advent, or Epiphany.

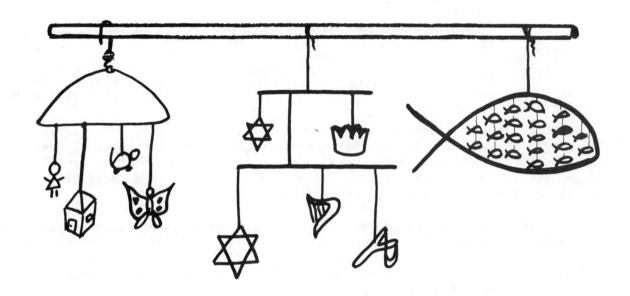

MAKE THINGS (crafts)

--- CAUTION ! ---

BE CAREFUL with crafts -- many projects, especially those recommended in some Vacation School manuals, are totally useless as far as educational value is concerned, and they are carried home by the children to become one more piece of religious debris. It must serve the lesson or it is a waste of time - whether or not the children enjoy it. Reread CHAPTER 1 of this book.

MAKE A PUPPET

Puppets can act out sacraments, biblical scenes, Christianity in daily life, and many more such themes. Do not rehearse dialogue--follow rules of creative drama. Puppetry is more versatile if the number of actors is small. Mention it as a possibility when you divide the children into small groups and allow them to choose their own project.

Puppets do not have to be people, and it is sometimes possible to have all children participate in a puppet project.

They can be quite elaborate, but it is better to keep them moderately simple when used in religion class.

To make simple stick puppets draw the figure on paper. If it is a person, dress with cloth scraps. Cut out. Paste on black paper. Cut out again, leaving 1/4" black border showing. Tape to a ruler or stick. Use a desk in a doorway as a stage.

Make puppets out of socks (stuff head, tie at neck, glue on features) or small paper bags (draw the features with magic-marker, paint, crayon, glue on construction paper or yarn hair, etc.) or small box (use paint-- add a little liquid detergent so it will stick, or construction paper to decorate). Make puppets totally out of cloth, or make the body of cloth and use a styrofoam ball for the head, or a papier-mache head.

<u>Have a puppet show of creation</u>.

   After lessons on creation, let each child make a simple puppet by
painting and cutting out a cardboard figure of water, sun, flowers, and
so forth; paste it on a flat stick or hang it on thin strings, so that
it can be manipulated. One child reads the Genesis account of creation,
while the others show it visually. This can be done as a "celebration"
or it can be shown to another class.

 <u>Have a play about "words</u>."

   Let the children write a play illustrating the fact that some words
unite people and other words separate people. The characters in the
play can ask the audience to give some of their ideas, too. End the
play by having the puppets lead everyone in singing "The more we get
together, together, together. The more we get together, the happier
we'll be. For your friends are my friends and my friends are your
friends. The more we get together the happier we'll be." (Tune of
"Did You Ever See a Lassie.")

 <u>Make a box to celebrate God's glory</u>.

   Discuss the word "glory"--what are some glorious colors, sounds,
ideas, activities. Why do we pray "Glory to God in the Highest"? What
is the glory of God? Cover small boxes (shoe boxes are good) with
glorious colors and pictures. This is a treasure box that the child
can take home to keep glorious possessions in. This is an especially
good lesson just before the summer break. When the boxes are finished,
arrange for the children to leave the room, and put some "surprises"
(erasers, candy, gold stars, marbles, rubber bands, hair ribbons,
mirrors, magnets, etc.) in the boxes to start their collection of trea-
sures.

 <u>Make a candle to celebrate Easter</u>.

   Paraffin can be heated and poured into a mold (milk carton, paper-
towel roll lined with aluminum foil, etc.). Then suspend a wick
(weighted with a paper clip or penny) over the center. (Tie it to a
pencil and rest it on the sides of the container.) Allow to dry; decorate with melted wax crayons, enamel paint, felt.

   The children get a smaller but more personal candle by hand dipping
it. Heat paraffin in a tall thin container (the candles will be as
tall as the depth of the wax in the container) and allow to cool somewhat. Each child dips his wick (weighted) into the wax and waits for
it to cool, then dips again. After 2 or 3 dips it will be strong
enough to remove the weight. The "greedy" child who leaves his candle
in too long will find that it comes out thinner than it went in. The
class could sing while taking turns at the container.

   Instead of paraffin you can melt down old candle stubs.

   The finished candles can be decorated, used in a "celebration."

<u>Build a model of the church of the future</u>
incorporating new changes in its design.

 <u>Build a model of the terrain of Palestine.</u>

 <u>Build a model of Jerusalem at the time of Christ.</u>

 <u>Make a set of vestments</u>
for use by one of the students at a demonstration of the Eucharist
or for use by the priest at a Mass planned by and for the class. These
need not be elaborate or permanent.

 <u>Sew a baptismal robe</u>
for a new brother or sister of one of the children in the class.
Discuss the meaning of baptism. Attend a baptism as a class.

THE ART CLOSET

An indispensable part of a successful religious education program is the
well stocked cupboard, from which the teacher, like a good scribe, pulls
out "things old and new." Art materials can be very expensive, but careful planning, some scrounging, and a sharp eye for substitutes will provide a very satisfactory supply shelf without forcing you to mortgage the
rectory.

Paint brushes and scissors are not the items on which to save money.
Cheap brushes do not paint satisfactorily and fall apart anyway. Good
brushes can last indefinitely when the children are taught to take care of
them--in other words, don't "scrub" with it, don't allow paint to harden
in it, etc. For inexpensive disposable "brushes" try cotton swabs, a
roll of cloth attached to a stick with a rubber band, the tip of a twig
("as is," or beaten with a hammer into a flexible pulp), and so on. Cheap
scissors do not cut, and are a great frustration, no matter how young the
children.

<u>ART CLOSET</u> (A minimum list)

    pencils
    colored chalk (vivid colors--look in a school or art supply store
        rather than a dime store)
    crayons
    felt-tip pens (wide and fine point, washable)
    tempera paint--cheaper in powder form, simple to mix
        basic colors: black, white, brown, red, blue, yellow,
                        orange, green, purple, magenta
    water colors
    liquid starch (mix with tempera for finger paint)
    soap flakes (mix with tempera for finger paint)

wheat paste (for papier-mache)
glue: Elmer's or Sobo, Polymer medium
brushes (from large round #12 on down)
sponges (for cleaning up, for painting)
scissors (have a few pairs of large ones for teachers)
clay (pre-moistened; the real McCoy, not the oil-base plasticene) or
    play-dough
cloth--large pieces for banners, etc. (see page 68) scraps for applique,
    etc.
yarn, thread, string, ribbon, wire
banner poles and standards (re-usable)
wire cutter
coat hangers
plastic tac
masking tape
scotch tape
pins
thumb tacks
magazines--old issues of Life, Look, Ebony are priceless; anything with
    good photos is helpful--stockholder annual reports, brochures, news
    magazines
bottles with screw tops (for mixing and keeping paint)

PAPER

newsprint--large sheets, rolls (ask a friend at a newspaper office for
    the end of the roll)
advertising paper--unused billboards donated by a local ad agency come
    in marvelous big sheets, in snappy colors, usable on blank or colored
    side
colored tissue--art paper (like Crystal Craft Tissue) not dime-store
    type package wrap.
shelf paper, butcher paper by the roll--for murals, magazine candid
construction paper--12" x 18" size
discarded gift wrap--solid and metallic colors
white art paper--better quality than newsprint--for special "productions"
    by the children
scratch, or "next to new"--get friends, parishioners, local businessmen
    to donate the paper that is ordinarily discarded in their offices or
    stores.
poster paper, tagboard
old newspapers--for papier-mache and collage and to protect the floor
    and table

SCRAP BOX

wood scraps, spools, felt--yarn--cloth scraps, paper plates, corrugated
    paper, sandpaper, leather, pieces of styrofoam, wire, metal foil,
    lace, egg cartons, etc., etc., etc.!

You can gather materials out-of-doors--lovely pebbles, pods, nuts, feathers

Try to see the possibilities in odds and ends, but DON'T just collect old holy cards, religious calendars, broken rosaries, armless statues, and other religious junk!

When someone gives you a large supply of something--FREE--ask a professional art teacher for ideas if you don't know how to use it.

OPTIONAL EQUIPMENT

brayer
glass
plaster of paris
waxed paper
old shirts and aprons (to protect clothing)

A portion of the first floor of the Boston, Massachusetts Children's Museum is devoted to a resource center. It contains a wealth of industrial by-products, surplus, and manufacturers' rejects, all of which can be used as materials for education. Rubber, foam rubber, plastic, styrofoam, wood, metal, paper, cardboard, fabric, lenses, and other materials, in a multitude of sizes, shapes, and colors can be obtained in two ways: 1) shoppers may fill a grocery bag with materials for $2.50, or, 2) groups, such as schools, classrooms, day care centers, Y's, or scouts, may become members for ten months by paying $10.00. They can then buy bagfulls of materials at half-price. The center offers workshops on specific uses of recycled materials.

Similar centers have been opened in other cities. Perhaps there is one near you. If not, start one yourself!!

BOOKS ON ARTS AND CRAFTS

Card and Cardboard. New York: Franklin Watts, Inc. Working with paper.

Cole, Natalie Robinson. The Arts in the Classroom. New York: John Day, 1940.

_____. Children's Art from Deep Down Inside. New York: John Day, 1966.

Gardner, Richard M. 101 Masks. New York: D. McKay Co., 1968.

Hawkinson, John and Martha Faulhaber. Music and Instruments for Children to Make. Music Involvement Series, Book One. Albert Whitman & Co.

Helena, Sr. M. Art Syllabus and Manual for Catholic Elementary Schools. Morristown: Silver Burdett, 1962.

Kampmann, Lothar. Creating with Found Objects. New York: Van Nostrand Reinhold, English edition, 1973.

Kennedy, Dorothea B. Crafts and Religious Symbols. Dayton: Pflaum, 1965.

Laliberte, Norman and Richey Kehl. 100 ways to have fun with an alligator & 100 other involving art projects. Blauvelt, New York: Art Education, 1969.

Let's See No. 1: The Use and Misuse of Visual Arts in Religious Education. Edited by Cella T. Hubbard. New York: Paulist Press, 1966.

Malcolm, Dorothea C. Art from Recycled Materials. Worcester, Massachusetts: Davis Publications; distributed by Sterling Publishing Co. of New York, 1974.

Romberg, Jenean. Let's Discover Paper. Let's Discover Watercolor. Let's Discover Mobiles. Let's Discover Tempera. Let's Discover Papier-Mache. Let's Discover Printing. Let's Discover Weaving. Let's Discover Tissue. Let's Discover Crayon. Let's Discover Puppets. Arts and Crafts Discovery Units. New York: The Center for Applied Research in Education, Inc., 1975.

Stevens, Harold. Ways with Art; 50 Techniques for Teaching Children. New York: Reinhold, 1963.

<u>School Arts</u>, Baltimore, Maryland. 10 issues annually; $7 per year. An
    art education magazine for teachers.

<u>Everyday Art</u>. Jersey City, New Jersey: The American Crayon Company.

Chapter 10: THE VISUAL ARTS (Slides, Filmstrips & Films)

SLIDES

Help your students sharpen their powers of observation and perception through
picture-taking. The Kodak Instamatic is an inexpensive, simple, and effi-
cient camera and would be a worthwhile investment for the parish or school.
Polaroid cameras offer the advantage of instant development--but the pictures
cannot be easily made into slides later. Ask one of the "camera-bugs" in
the parish for help if you don't know which end to look through--but don't
get too complicated. Experience is the best teacher.

 Make a slide presentation of the call of the apostles.
    Children take the parts of the biblical characters and pose for a
series of snapshots that will tell the story when shown in sequence.
They can dress in costume, and simulate fishermen, tax collector and
other details, or better, translate those jobs and persons into contemporary terms (Peter and Andrew might have been miners or construction workers, Matthew would have been a regional director of the I.R.S.).
The narration can be taped or given live as the slides are presented.

 Make a "news report" on your local scene.
    Walk with a group of older students through the poorest section of
your town. Let them shoot pictures with their cameras. Later ask
them to write down how they felt, how it was different from just passing through on some other occasion. Display the pictures taken on the
walk; discuss them, and the quality of life they portray.

    Slides can also be made by lifting a picture from a magazine with clear
contact-adhesive shelving paper. The method is simple and can be used suc-
cessfully even by seven-year-olds. Use a cardboard slide mount (available
at camera and hobby stores) as a frame, to find part of a magazine picture
(approximately 1½" square) which will look good as a slide. Next, press a
piece of transparent contact paper about 2" square over the chosen picture.
Rub it hard with the bottom of a spoon or other hard, smooth object. When
the contact paper and the picture are well attached to each other, cut it
out and soak it in warm water. In a short time the paper on which the picture was printed will peel away, leaving the ink stuck to the contact paper.
Wipe off any remains of the original paper, cover the back with another
piece of contact paper if it is sticky, trim it to the exact size of the
cardboard slide mount, seal the mount with a warm iron, and your slide is
ready for the projector. Slides made in this way have a coarse, grainy
look--which has its own kind of charm.

Make a "family of man" slide presentation.

Lift several dozen magazine pictures of people--concentrate on faces. Be sure to include a wide range of races, activities, groupings, ages, nationalities, and so forth.

 Make a "film strip" of creation.

The first section would include the works of nature such as flowers, sunset, water, mountains, rocks, insects--whatever can be found in your supply of magazines which will fit the small scale of the mounts. The second section, which shows the ways in which men and women share in the work of the Creator, can include pictures of shoes, buildings, handcrafts of all kinds, cooked food, factory production lines, etc. A reading from the first and second chapters of Genesis would be an appropriate narration, or the Psalm of the Young Men in the Fiery Furnace ("Fire and ice bless the Lord") could be rewritten to accommodate the slides selected.

FILMSTRIPS

Filmstrips (and slides) can easily be made in the classroom through use of a specially treated strip of plastic film made the size of a standard 35 mm single frame filmstrip--sprocketed and ready for threading into a filmstrip projector. The students simply draw, type or print their message directly on the film, being careful to stay within each "framed" area. The finished product can be sprayed with a fixative or erased and re-used later. This non-photographic production of filmstrips requires no special equipment, only colored projection pencils or felt-tip pens (the kind used for overhead transparencies) or India inks. The treated film is available in kits, or alone at very reasonable prices. A filmstrip yields 16 frames per foot. It is recommended that your initial purchase be a kit, as the set of instructions and suggestions, as well as the cardboard holder, are very helpful. Splicers are also available. Children can also use outdated acetate filmstrips which have been recycled by removing the picture emulsion with a chlorine bleach solution.

This activity is suitable for intermediate and older children who enjoy working on small pictures (each frame is just over a square inch) and who can think in terms of sequence and illustration. Abstract designs and words can be used of course, as well as pictures. It is a simple technique, does not require lengthy preparation or expensive processing or bulky equipment. Mistakes can be erased, and individual students or committees or teachers can produce each filmstrip and have the pleasure of seeing their own work projected on the screen. It is a good medium for the culmination of a unit, or for deepening and interpretive activities for non-writers.

To make a slide presentation, simply cut off each frame and seal it in a standard cardboard slide mount.

These materials are available under the following trade names, at the addresses listed, as well as at most large school supply houses.

U-Film (or U-Write-on-Film)   Prima Educational Products
A Division of Hudson Photographic
   Industries, Inc.
Irvington-on-Hudson, New York 10533

Do-It-Yourself Filmstrip/   Valiant I.M.C.
  Slide Kits   195 Bonhomme Street
Hackensack, New Jersey 07062

Rite-On Kits   Bro-Dart Eastern Division
1609 Memorial Avenue
Williamsport, Pennsylvania 17701

Starex Stripette Film Kits   Josten's Library Supplies
4070 Shirley Drive, S.W.
Atlanta, Georgia 38336

Develop a story about Abner Apostle.
After studying the Acts of the Apostles, and learning the general pattern of the early development of the churches, ask the class to work out a story (or series of stories) of a mythical thirteenth apostle. Where did he travel, how was he received, what was his message, how did he present it, what was the reaction of the listeners, what happened next, did he move on, what happened after he left, how did he answer certain questions, what were the concerns of the people? How can these events be visualized?

Students can divide the work on the narrative, maps showing his travels, drawings of the characters. Drawings should be kept simple, e.g. stick figures, line drawings similar to those of the American Bible Society, or faces without bodies.

Develop a story about Peter Penitent.
Why does Peter want to receive the sacrament of reconciliation, how does he prepare, what does the priest say, what does he do, what does Peter respond?

Develop a Thanksgiving filmstrip.
Let each child use three or four frames to draw the people and events and things for which he or she is grateful. Show the finished strip as part of a prayer celebration.

Draw a year-end review.
The students can present their understanding and memory of the studies of the year in filmstrip or slide form, accompanied by original narrative which can include passages from their text books or the Bible.

FILMS

Making an 8 mm film is relatively easy--people have been making "home movies"
for years. While shooting a story is more complicated than merely collect-
ing a visual record of family vacations and birthday parties, it is still
as simple as ABCD!--and not as expensive as you think.

A. Write a script (or "shooting schedule").
    What is the theme, event, or story you want to picture? If it
    is a story, what details are essential and relevant? What scenes
    or shots can communicate the situation to the viewer? Jot down
    as many possibilities as you can, then eliminate those that are
    impractical to organize (for example, an automobile accident) or
    for which you do not have the necessary equipment (shots requir-
    ing a zoom lens).

    If you are going to have actors, involve them in this process
    of preparation, so that they are able to help think out the stag-
    ing with you. This will help them act more naturally and feel
    more a part of the film.

    The actual "script" may be as detailed or general as you like.
    It can be a diagram of each scene, showing the movement of the
    actors, necessary lighting, indication of close-up and distance
    shots, special effects, symbolic shots, and so on. It should at
    least remind you of all the marvelous ideas you had during your
    "think sessions" so that you don't forget to shoot them. It
    should spell out the action and mood of the scenes enough to help
    the actors perform smoothly and eliminate unnecessary reshooting
    of scenes (which is expensive, time-consuming, and generally dif-
    ficult to organize). You can take Polaroid or other snapshots
    of the actors and scenes to help your planning. These preview
    stills will show what your scene looks like to the camera eye.

B. Plan the sound.
    Silent films can be accompanied by an instrumental recording of
    classical music selected according to the theme of the picture.
    If this is your plan, do not worry further about a sound "script."
    It is also simple enough to write a narration and/or sound effects
    and/or dialogue which can be put on a tape recorder, to be played
    as the picture is shown. In this case it is easier to make the
    film first and then record the sound track as you watch the edited
    film on the screen, so that your timing is correct. It is also
    possible, but more complicated, to record the sound first. In
    either case, the narration and sound effects should be planned in
    advance of shooting scenes to that allowance can be made for the
    length of time it takes to say something. If all this becomes
    too complicated, forget it and just let your "camera crew" make
    the film their eyes tell them to make. The general rule in reli-
    gious education should be remembered: the procedure should not
    claim so much attention that the children forget the religious
    meaning of their work.

The recent development of sound equipment for the home movie market puts "talkies" within reach of every classroom. It is not difficult to write a dialogue for simple stories, but it is probably easier to prepare the actors to ad lib as they go. If actors make a mistake, or if a scene is edited after it has been photographed, you will find gaps and unfinished sentences on your sound track. To correct this simply erase and re-record it. In fact in many cases it is easier to plan to do the final sound track after the picture is complete. Synchronizing the dialogue with lip movements is very difficult to achieve so just do the best you can. You will also be able to introduce background music, special sound effects, etc. You can also rewrite your narration to accommodate unexpected changes which occur during shooting.

C. Shoot your film.
   Don't be afraid to take more scenes than you think you will need. You never quite know what you have captured on film until you see it developed. Only about one-third of all the film you expose is used in the final version of the movie, so go ahead and take the shots that occur to you while "on location." Scenes need not be shot in the order which they will have in the final movie, because you can cut film and rearrange the sequence. It takes time to set up a scene and take it carefully, so don't be in a rush. You can edit your film later, but you can't change it--so think about the details.

   Use black and white or colored film depending on the mood of your movie. Use high or low speed depending on the amount of light available. Do you want the strong shadows thrown by a light bar or do you want to use natural light only?

   Send your film to a competent processor. Film can be ruined by careless developing.

D. Edit the movie.
   Cut out the pieces of film that you don't like, or that seem to drag things out too long. Splice the pieces you want together. Save all the pieces of good film that you cut out--you might want to use them on some other movie.

PREPARATION

Talk it over with the students before deciding on the project. It ordinarily does not take much to motivate them but they should certainly have the freedom to choose not to make a movie. A film is a very time-consuming and personal production, and, like anything creative, should not be forced. Students can work individually, in groups, or the whole class can work on a single production.

Invite a teenager or young adult who has made movies to show some to your students and discuss with them the techniques he or she used. This is especially important if you have never done one.

Be well acquainted with your equipment before starting, of course. Read the manual thoroughly, get some pointers from an experienced friend, and shoot some experimental film of your own before introducing the project to the students. Then conduct a class on the use of the equipment--discuss the ASA numbers, shutter speeds, method of loading, distance gauge, and any other factors that are important to the operation of the particular camera you and your students will use. Many simple home cameras are practically foolproof, and you might be able to borrow several for this project. Let the students shoot several rolls of film for practice. This adds to your total expense but many students who hold the camera steady and do everything correctly when practicing with an empty camera will "freeze" when they try to take a scene they really want.

Practice editing when your practice rolls are developed. You can also obtain TV newsfilms that the station is ready to throw away. They can be used for observation of camera techniques before using them for cutting and splicing.

AFTER THIS PREPARATION, IT IS AS EASY AS

    A. WRITE THE SCRIPT

       B. PLAN THE SOUND

          C. SHOOT THE FILM

             D. EDIT THE MOVIE

A word on the adult's role in the student film

There are several ways to approach your working relationship with the young film-makers. You may want to act as moderator and co-author with them by sharing in the creative process, working out each scene with the group step by step. This is suitable if the group will produce one film rather than a film per student. If each student, or several small teams are working on individual movies, it is better if the adult does not become an acting member of each team--since the teacher too easily out-talks or out-votes the partners. You might then assume the role of technical assistant--available for consultation but not calling the shots.

In any case, the movie will be the "teacher's thing" if the teacher acts as the authoritarian producer-director with all the ideas and skills and decisions. This defeats the whole purpose of making the film.

SOME FILM SUGGESTIONS:

 A documentary on the "Caring Community."

Doctors, police, cafeteria aides, ushers, teachers, grocers and hundreds of other persons contribute to our individual and communal well-being. As part of their study of community helpers or Christian commitment or works of love, each child or small committee can shoot three or four scenes of such persons on the job. All are then spliced together into a giant documentary. A taped interview with the workers or sound effects from the job or a taped explanation of the Christian dimension of the job could be used as the sound track. (This idea is also suitable for a slide presentation or album of snapshots.)

 A creative review project.

Ask the students to present a 50-foot movie (i.e. one roll of film) suggested to them by the unit just finished. They should work in small committees of four to six students. You might want to specify that they present their film unedited, so that they will keep things simple.

 A modern parable.

Ask the students to transpose a parable of Jesus into a modern situation which is its equivalent.

 Film a meaningful song.

Using a popular or religious song as a sound track, make a film that conveys a message or mood.

 A film on reconciliation.

Ask the students to make a film on the subject of Christian reconciliation using symbols only--no human actors.

 A film essay.

Ask the students to write essays on "recognizing Christ in the modern world," "what my faith means to me," or "the meaning of Confirmation." Select the best or the one with good imagery or work out a composite of the class writings. Then ask the children to make a film based on that script.

 A sacramental film.

Ask the students to make a film on baptism or first communion or marriage. The film should start with the preparations in the home and at the school and church, the gathering of the participants, vesting of the celebrant, the actual ceremony, festivities after the liturgy. The students can stage all these scenes or shoot an actual event.

BOOKS AND PAMPHLETS THAT MAY BE HELPFUL

Andersen, Yvonne. Make Your Own Animated Movies; Yellow Ball Workshop
    Film Techniques. Boston: Little, Brown, & Co., 1970.

_____. Teaching Film Animation to Children. New York: Van Nostrand,
    1970.

Classroom Projects Using Photography. Part I: For the Elementary School
    Level. Rochester, New York: Eastman Kodak Co., 1975.

Home Movies Made Easy. Rochester, New York: Eastman Kodak Co., 1974. Kodak
    Publication No. AD-5.

How to Make Good Sound Movies. Rochester, New York: Eastman Kodak Co., 1976.
    Kodak Publication No. AD-2.

Kuhns, William. Exploring the Film. Dayton: Geo. A. Pflaum, 1968. Good
    background on the film as art, some technical help in film-making.

Lidstone, John & McIntosh, Don. Children As Film Makers. New York: Van
    Nostrand, 1970.

Lowndes, Douglas. Film Making in Schools. New York: Watson-Guptill Publi-
    cations, 1968.

Picarus, Edward. Guide to Filmmaking. New York: Signet. Paperback.

Schneider, Kent & Ortegel, Adelaide. Light: A Language of Celebration.
    Chicago: Center for Contemporary Celebration, 1973.

Suid, Murray. Painting with the Sun: A First Book of Photography. Boston:
    CSCS, Inc., 1970.

SEE ALSO: Specialized magazines such as The American Cinematographer, Modern
    Photography, and The Independent Filmmaker; they will keep you up-to-
    date on the latest developments in film techniques and technology.

Information on technical problems, as well as pamphlets on film-making, are
    available from Eastman Kodak, Rochester, New York. Your local camera
    stores are also a source of information and guidance.

. . . to stimulate life,

      leaving it then free to develop, to unfold,

herein lies the first task of the educator . . .

                             M. Montessori

Chapter 11: EXPERIENCE

The classroom is an artificial environment. It has been created so that individuals can stand aside from daily concerns in order to look at them objectively--reflect on them, learn from the insights of others into these realities--and so be better equipped to act with sound judgment when no longer in the classroom environment.

It is the teacher's role to select aspects of life (now one, now another) and introduce them into the classroom somehow, for the reflection of the students.

To do this the teacher employs many skills, techniques, materials, and equipment. Many of these have been mentioned elsewhere in this book.

However, there is a whole category of student-involvement activities which can only be described as "experiences." This includes demonstrations, simulations, field trips, prayer experiences, and multi-media "happenings."

1. DEBATE, PANEL DISCUSSION

    These activities help students look at an event or issue from more than one point of view. They require a certain amount of maturity and outside preparation, and the students may need help in developing the necessary skills. For best results topics which are genuinely open-ended should be chosen for debate. This means that no one is put into the position of defending a position which is patently evil (e.g. "Resolved, that all laws against murder be abolished.") or which does not allow for much creativity (e.g. a panel discussion on "why we should love our parents").

 Have a debate on renewal in the liturgy.
    Choose an affirmative and a negative team to debate: "Resolved, that church buildings should be sold and the Eucharist (or Sunday service) celebrated only in private homes."

 Have a panel discussion on renewal in the liturgy.
    Ask several children to think about forms of liturgical worship they consider most suitable for our times, and present their ideas to the class. After the presentation, time should be allowed for questions and answers, and then discussion in small groups (5 to 8 persons).

2. CREATIVE DEMONSTRATIONS

 Demonstrate the old and new covenant worship.

Divide the children into two teams. The first recreates the Tent of Meeting. They can set up a tent out-of-doors, curtain off an area for the Holy of Holies, supply the needed furniture, dishes, and so on. The second group sets up a model of the church--altar, chalice, pulpit. The models can be as simple or as complex as the children's research, imagination, and talent dictate.

 Demonstrate the call of the apostles.

The children sit quietly in a circle on the floor. One by one the teacher whispers each child's name. When called, the child comes, receives a personal message or greeting from the teacher, and remains there until all are "called" by name and given a personal welcome. Suitable for young children, a simple ceremony but with a genuine "sacramental" dimension. Could be concluded by joining hands and singing an appropriate song. (See "We are All the Lord's Apostles" in Chapter 2.)

 Demonstrate the effects of disunity.

Ask students to stand in a circle with joined hands (sign of unity). Ask them to imagine that a quarrel begins, and because of it the class breaks up into two (or more) separate groups. Each group should move as far away from the others as possible in the classroom. Then assign a task for which cooperation would normally be expected, such as asking the children to make a single mural depicting the teachings of Christ. The only rule imposed is that no one may communicate in any way with the members of another group until the mural is finished. While the children are working the teacher should not mediate, intervene, or interfere.

After the mural is complete the students discuss the difficulties of working without communication and its partner, cooperation, and the disappointing results of the mural (presumably it will not be as good as they are capable of). Then the teacher explains: their split represents the break-down of the Church into "denominations" which for many centuries has prevented the followers of Christ from working together to live and proclaim His teachings.

3. FIELD TRIPS

 Visit neighboring churches and synagogues.

 Visit a bakery.
As part of a unit on the Eucharist--bread as a fitting sign, and so forth.

 Visit places in the community where the Spirit is active.
The state legislature, the mayor's office, the jail, the local factories and businesses, the hospitals--wherever men and women are trying to build a Christian city and world. Especially good for junior high and older, as part of preparation for confirmation.

4. PRAYER EXPERIENCES

NB: To pray is to raise one's mind and heart to God--to meet Him in friendship and trust, to listen attentively, to speak from the abundance of one's heart. It is genuine communication. It was an error of the past several generations to think that the proper way to initiate children into the habit of prayer was to have them learn certain "essential" prayers as rapidly and as correctly as possible. This task of memorization was even considered the criterion by which their readiness to receive the Body of Christ was judged.

In recent years every effort is being made to direct children (and adults) toward a spirit of prayer which includes more spontaneity, a scriptural foundation, a liturgical direction, and a clearer relationship to daily life. For further reading on this subject, the reader is directed to such journals as The Living Light, The Catechist, Religious Education, Religion Teacher's Journal, and Bringing Religion Home.

Prayer experiences can be very simple . . .

★ Appreciate God's providence (Plan A).
     Each child draws a picture of something or someone in his life
through which (whom) God's love and care is apparent. Across their
pictures the children then write "Great is His love, love without end."
They hang their pictures, learn to sing Psalm 135, using that antiphon
(Gelineau, Twenty-Four Psalms and a Canticle).

★ Appreciate God's providence (Plan B).
     Sing "Now Thank We All Our God" (People's Mass Book, World Library
of Sacred Music), with suitable gestures (see page 25).

. . . or more elaborate!

★ Pray an original "Way of the Cross."
     Divide the children into teams. Ask them to think of the meaning
of each "station." Ask them to discuss the ways in which Christ is
experiencing that same reality today--and make a collage of magazine
pictures, newspaper headlines, and so on (or use a single strong picture) illustrating that reality. Hang the student illustrations beside
each station in the church. Have them write up a Way of the Cross
ceremony, invite other classes to share it with them. One of the students, or the priest, can lead it, flanked by candle and cross bearers.
(Contemporary visuals and prayers for a student Way of the Cross are
available. They are excellent, but the benefit of the students creating their own meditations should not be sacrificed for the more professional polish that a commercial set provides.)

Prayer experiences can be informal . . .

★ Share your reason for praying.
     After a brief period of silent reflection, the children mention to
each other the intentions they would like everyone to pray for. When
everyone who would like to offer an intention has done so, the leader
reads from Scripture or leads the Lord's Prayer.

. . . or ritualized!

★ Make up a litany on loneliness.
     After discussing loneliness in his experience (try to draw all of
the students beyond stereotyped answers), each child writes a phrase
for the litany. They are compiled, duplicates eliminated, polished,
mimeographed for use in the next class, or as an offertory petition
litany at the liturgy.

★ Make a visualized litany on the call of the Christian.
     Each student finds a magazine picture symbolic of the way in which
God is calling to the Christian to do or be something. Each student
(standing in a circle, prayerful atmosphere) holds up his or her picture

for all to see, saying, "Lord, you have called us to . . . (stop wars, feed the hungry of the Sahel, talk to old people who are lonely--whatever his picture suggests). All of the students respond (as the prophets responded), "Speak, Lord, for your servants are listening."

5. MULTI-MEDIA EVENTS

Each class period or unit of material makes use of many art forms and activities, in order to vary the pace and impact of the hour or week or season. However, a multi-media event uses several kinds of activity or experience at the same time to build a single theme, to leave a single impression upon the participant.

 Enjoy a morning of sharing.
The teacher begins the period of preparation with a reading of The Three Robbers by Tomi Ungerer (Atheneum) and conversation about the talents (symbolized by the chest of gold in the story) that lie buried in each of us. Then the students prepare something of their own to share with one of the residents of a home for the aged. It can be a song to sing, an original story to read, a collection of rocks or postcards to show, an album of pictures, a science experiment or a ballet routine to demonstrate. The important thing is that each child have something personal to share and talk about. They will also be reminded that the person with whom they will share the morning has lived a long and interesting life, and has a treasure chest of memories to share in return. The persons at the home who wish to participate in the "morning of sharing" will be told in advance what to expect from the children, and asked to think of something they would like to tell about or show.

The morning of sharing itself begins with a showing of the film-strip of The Three Robbers (Weston Woods), followed by a reading of the parable of the talents and a very short homily on the talents that we each have hidden carefully away. Next each child, or a small group of two or three meets with an older person and shares whatever has been prepared. After about 15 or 20 minutes the entire group gathers once again for a snack and a song.

In this case the four media (film, prayer, talent, food) are not used similtaneously, but as parts of a single visit or party.

 Plan a sight-sound-action event on the theme of bread.
Students form three committees. The first prepares a series of slides showing all kinds of bread, hungry or starving persons, bakeries, wheat, ovens full of muffins, bags of flour, sandwiches, sweetrolls, persons eating bread, etc. The second group prepares a tape recording (with or without background music) of scripture readings on bread, such as Jesus feeding the multitude, the last supper, manna in the desert,

the first temptation, etc. The third group prepares a pantomime-dance on the same topic, not "acting out" but interpreting the feeding of the multitude, the giving/receiving of holy communion, the feeding of the hungry of the world, etc.

The three groups work somewhat independently, but knowing that all three parts will be presented simultaneously. The event is then presented (for themselves only or for another class, parents, etc.) in a prayerful, meditative fashion.

6. SIMULATION EVENTS

These activities imitate real life; the closer the experiences can come to actual events the more they will be able to communicate a new point of view to the students. These are exercises planned to help Christians reevaluate their understandings and priorities, to "walk a mile in the other's moccasins."

Hold a hunger day.
Plan a day of prayer, education and solidarity for older children and their parents during which the meals will be very sparse--bread and water for breakfast, bread and a single piece of fruit for lunch. For dinner serve an elegant meal of chicken, rice and vegetable to 10% of the participants, rice and a hot dog to another 30% and rice only to the rest, to simulate the unequal distribution of the world's food resources.

Be discriminating.
Simulate discrimination in order to appreciate its effect upon both those who are discriminated against and those who are part of the privileged group. First select a group arbitrarily, such as those who wear glasses or are left handed, and then develop a situation which will isolate and demean them. For example, announce that the minority group will only be able to use designated water fountains and bathrooms and chairs (in the back of the classroom). As the day wears on they also discover that teachers never call on them, they get smaller helpings in the cafeteria, etc.

This project should be used only with students who are old enough to understand its purpose and implications, and should be organized by moderators who are able to deal with the hostility it sometimes causes.

Play a simulation game.
Each student draws a sealed envelope of "money" with which to purchase food and building materials. The object of the game is to build the most beautiful house possible in one "year" (36 minutes). The only rule is that at the beginning of each month (3 minutes, called by timekeeper) each player must acquire another food unit or "starve" (drop out of the game). Food units costing $1.00 are on a table, along

with building materials priced as follows: roofing units (black paper) $1.00; siding for $5.00, $3.00, and $1.00 (bright paper, brown paper and newspaper respectively); glue for $3.00 per bottle. These materials can be as simple or elaborate as you wish to provide, priced according to desirability.

Money has been put in the envelopes according to the following formula for each ten students: $400, $250, $150, $125, $100, $50, $5, $5, $5. As the children play they will discover the wide variety in resources. Let the game continue until the year is up or the students with enough money complete their houses. The "have nots" may borrow, steal, improvise--let them work it out the best they can, but once they are out of food two months they are out of the game.

After the game hold a discussion. Ask the students how they enjoyed it, how the "have nots" felt, whether they had to drop out of the game early, whether people with lots of money found themselves building larger or fancier houses, how they responded when they found neighbors in need, etc. The students may have guessed that they represent peoples of the world who have varying amounts of natural resources. Relate their experience to the way nations deal with one another. How do poor nations feel? Is life a "fair" game? What problems besides hunger and lack of money do nations have? What are some solutions to these problems?

CHRIST SAID, I COME TO MAKE ALL THINGS NEW !!

Creativity is an exquisitely human faculty that is essential not only
              for each person's individual growth, but for the
                       evolution of all humankind.

It grows out of the uniqueness of the individual.
      It grows out of the use of and response to materials, events,
                       people, and circumstances in life.
          Its mainspring seems to be our tendency to actualize ourselves
                       to become our potentialities.

The creative act is always a process interrelating the person and the world.
          It is essential to the formation of an integrated person.

It is taking part of something outside of oneself and giving it new life
              from within oneself.
      It is giving that new life to the world.

It is taking all the growth we gain through our awareness of creation
                  and making something new from our own being.

Creative people change their world, they change others.
          They create an atmosphere in which others may grow and give.

Any activity of any person can have aspects of creativity about it.
      Creativity requires an openness to revealing one's fears, hopes,
          aches, loneliness, awkwardness, love.

Creativity means caring about everything

                              and

                          everyone.

      It means transforming everything we touch!

110

Chapter 12: CELEBRATION

A "celebration" is a special kind of prayer-experience. It holds the same relation to routine classroom prayers that the celebration of the Eucharist holds to daily meal blessing in the family. That is, it is a special, communal, ceremonial prayer. It is a statement of faith involving the body, mind, emotions and relationships, rather than an explanation or lesson or performance.

Since it is through the liturgy that Christians most often hear the Word of God proclaimed, and most consciously commit themselves to that Word, it is important that children be led to an understanding of corporate worship. The liturgy or the public worship of the Christian community uses visible things (bread, water, oil) and gestures (blessings, bowing, singing, laying on of hands) to convey an inner attitude of faith. Because it is multi-dimensional, the liturgy can address Christians on the perceptual, emotional, symbolic, intellectual, social and religious levels at once, and draw them beyond a merely intellectual grasp of doctrine to a faith commitment to the living God.

By celebrating in a variety of ways, we help children learn that God has not rigidly defined the manner in which He is to be worshipped. By celebrating the realities of everyday life, we help children learn that the liturgical year does not exhaust, but is only a skeleton of the possibilities for prayerful conversation with God. By involving children in the designing of various celebrations, we help them learn the dynamics of communal prayer, and we prepare a generation of worshippers who will be able to participate in renewing the liturgical forms within the churches.

When catechists first became interested in this whole area, the formula used was rather rigid: song, Scripture, song, Scripture, homily, rite, prayer, song (see below: "Celebrate Creation," Plan A). These were called Bible vigils. Teachers today see the need for incorporating art work, creative writing, drama, dance, song, choral reading, movies, magazine candids, and so on into these new forms of prayer. In fact, anything real, that is, significant and personal, has a place in worship. Celebration is not "theater" since there is no audience; everyone participates, though some may have a special duty or ministry to perform during the service. A catechetical celebration can be, in some cases, a more satisfying prayer event for children than the normal Sunday religious service because the theme and ceremonies are designed according to their interests and capacities, because they are never the same, and because the atmosphere can be very joyful and even playful. Children sometimes feel that they cannot be joyful at a regular service without showing disrespect.

111

Theme: something significant in the children's lives; simple, clear, real. The ceremony can be aimed at evoking joy, penitence, fellowship in Christ, or other Christian attitude, but should always begin and end with thanksgiving. As the ancient eucharistic prayer states, "Father, all-powerful and ever-living God, we do well always and everywhere to give you thanks through Jesus Christ our Lord."

Image: a symbol of the reality being celebrated; a visual sign or action that can help convey meaning and at the same time be itself part of the prayer; often taken from nature (planting seeds to symbolize God's promise of new life), everyday life (making banners with pictures of parents to help celebrate God's own care and parenting) or the liturgy (sprinkling water after renewing baptismal commitments). The image chosen may suggest rituals or art expressions or special location. Students should be involved in the development of the imagery of the celebration, since they have a good sense of symbol and because it is essential that the celebration be their own prayer and not just that of the adult teacher.

Readings: from scripture, children's books, poetry, newspapers, original works, lyrics of hymns or songs.

Music: religious or popular, selected according to the theme and the ability of all participants to sing along.

Ritual: an action of some sort; can be as simple as a deep bow to show reverence to the Bible as the Word of God, or as elaborate as a passion play; often echos the rituals of the liturgy (lighting small tapers from a "Christ" candle, sharing bread). Processions are popular, and the lighting of candles helps to establish an atmosphere of specialness and dignity. It should not be forgotten that silence for prayer or reflection is itself a ritual and is a very important element of Christian worship.

Environment: church or chapel, out-of-doors, around the baptismal font, or other special place; when held in the classroom some special things should be done to make the atmosphere and event different from other classroom prayers—desks can be cleared away, a special prayer-corner set aside, banners hung, candles lighted, etc. The use of student art work in vestments, banners, altar hangings, etc. is helpful because creating the artifacts helps to prepare them for the event, and use in a religious ceremony underlines the fact that the work of their own hands is consecrated to the Lord.

SOME CELEBRATION IDEAS:

 Celebrate the Church Unity Octave   (to be used at the Eucharist or other worship service).

    Each grade studies a different religion. Each class writes one petition regarding this faith to be used during the Prayers of the Faithful; the sung response to these petitions should be "God the Father hear our prayer" from Fr. Rivers' An American Mass Program. One group makes a large Chi Rho or other symbol of Christ to be placed upright at the center of the altar steps. At the offertory each grade brings a giant paper-chain link on which is written the name of the faith that was studied. One child staples them together as they are brought up, making a chain which is then hung on the Chi Rho. All people united in Christ.

 Celebrate the Passover.

    Ask several children to do research on the Passover meal and explain its meaning and ceremonies to the class. Then let the class plan a Passover-like celebration for themselves. Include suitable readings such as Exodus, Joshua, parts of the Haggadah, Christ's blessing prayers from the Last Supper, prayers of consecration of the eucharist (Roman Catholic), etc. The Seder plate, wine goblet, menorah and other special equipment can be borrowed, or made of papier-mache. Use real matzoh or let some students bake unleavened bread. This ceremony is especially suitable for Holy Thursday, or groups who are preparing for their first reception of communion, and it can be as simple or elaborate as is feasible.

Celebrate creation (Plan A).

Children's art work portraying various aspects of creation is displayed. All sing Psalm 99, while the leader (an adult), flanked by two candle-bearers, places the Bible on a stand prepared for it and bows deeply. The candles are placed beside the Book.

1st Reader:	"The Lord be with you."
All:	"And also with you."
1st Reader:	"A reading from the Book of Genesis, Chapter 1."
Leader:	"Glory be to God. Amen."
All:	"Glory be to God. Amen."
Leader:	"Let us sit down. Let us listen and open our hearts to the Word of God."
1st Reader:	(Genesis 1, vv. 1-8.)
All:	Sing meditation song: "There was an evening, there was a morn and God saw that it was good."
	Repeat.

(2nd, 3rd, 4th, and 5th readers read Genesis 1, vv. 9-13; Genesis 1, vv. 14-19; Genesis 1, vv. 20-25; and Genesis 1, vv. 26-28 respectively; the meditation song is repeated after each reading.)

Leader:	Homily (3 minutes)
	"Let us stand now and join our hearts to the prayer of one of us who is going to address our Heavenly Father in our name."
Child:	"Let us pray" (moment of silence).
	"Truly it is good and right, It is our duty, It is our salvation,
	To thank you always and everywhere
	Lord, Father Almighty, creator of heaven and earth.
	Through Jesus Christ our Lord
	You have created and still re-create all your marvelous creation in a new creation,
	Having blessed it, you have given it to man,
	Therefore, having received from you our human dignity and responsibility,
	With a joyful heart we sing your great Glory."
All:	Sing "Canticle of the Three Children."
	"May the Almighty Father, Creator of heaven and earth, bless you and keep you in His love."
All:	Sing "Amen."
	Sing Psalm 135 as leader and candle-bearers remove Bible and candles and leave in procession.

<u>Celebrate creation (Plan B)</u>.

In the classroom: make one mural that is divided in four parts or four murals. Let the children cut out and paste their own pictures.

1.	adults children babies fun work	2.	animals zoo food	3.	plants flowers trees fruit vines	4.	rocks mountains moon stars

Make up suitable praises to be sung later (for example, "For the shining sun above us, Father in heaven we thank you." "For apples and bananas, Father in heaven we thank you.") A simple chant tone will do, or use the melody and chorus of "Bless the Lord" by Clarence Rivers.

Form a procession to church with mural(s) singing Psalm 135. "O Give thanks to the Lord for He is good."
Place murals on altar or around sanctuary.
Sing praises children made up in classroom (all stand with folded hands and bow as they say ". . . thank you").
Silent meditation: Thank God for a special gift.
Process out singing: "Now thank we all our God."

 <u>Celebrate Mother's Day</u>   (to be used at the Eucharist or other service).

All children make things for their mothers to wear (crown of paper flowers, corsage of real flowers, joyful name tag or badge, etc.). Have balloons and signs ("Mom's the Word," "Parent Power") and banners for everyone to carry in procession. Have Mass out-of-doors. Choose Scripture readings and hymns appropriate to the day. Make a statue of Mary, the Christian symbol of motherhood (and don't carry an old one-- let the children carry one <u>they</u> made!) for the procession.

Tell the children to begin their celebration before they even get to church--bring Mother breakfast in bed, surprise her with some flowers, and so on. Plan with Father so the whole family celebrates together.

(For more details, see <u>Catechist</u>, May 1969, "Exchange" column.
George A. Pflaum, Inc.)

 <u>Celebrate your senses</u>.

As part of the celebration, have something to smell (burn incense, have flowers), taste (break bread, cake), touch (cool water, make a texture collage), hear (music, readings), and see (a film or magazine candid, a dance). Choose appropriate Scripture or other readings (Marshall McLuhan, etc.).

Celebrate Advent.
    Design a celebration using a reading of Isaiah 12:1-6, a litany or choral reading adapted from Isaiah 63:7-19, the song "O Come, O Come Immanuel," and the planting of a bulb in a dish of wet gravel (we <u>wait</u> for it to flower; try to find a bulb that will flower in four weeks if possible).

 Celebrate our solidarity with the poor.
    Invite the families of the parish or congregation to fast each Monday (or whatever day is convenient for the group), then gather in the evening for worship and a simple meal of a bowl of rice or noodles. The money saved is brought along and contributed to a fund for the feeding of the poor in some part of the world.

RESOURCES FOR RELIGIOUS CELEBRATIONS

Books

Belgium, Harold J. <u>Great Days for the Family</u>. St. Louis: Concordia Publishing House, 1969.

Bryce, Mary Charles. "Resource Bibliography for Liturgies with Young Christians." <u>Living Light</u>, Vol. 12, No. 3, Fall 1975, pp. 461-467.

Bucher, Janet. <u>Run with Him</u>. Cincinnati: North American Liturgy Resources, 1973.

Caprio, Betsy. <u>Experiments in Prayer</u>. Notre Dame: Ave Maria Press, 1973.

<u>Children's Liturgies</u>. ed. Virginia Sloyan & Gabe Huck. Washington, D.C.: The Liturgical Conference, 1970.

Faucher, Thomas Neiland, Ione. <u>Touching God</u>. Notre Dame: Ave Maria Press, 1975.

Freburger, William J. and Haas, James E. <u>Eucharistic Prayers for Children with Twenty Suggested Liturgies</u>. Notre Dame: Ave Maria Press, 1976.

Haas, James E. <u>Shout Hooray: Contemporary Celebrations</u>. New York: Morehouse-Barlow, 1973.

_____ and Haas, Lynne. <u>Make a Joyful Noise!</u> New York: Morehouse-Barlow, 1973.

Haas, James E. <u>Praise the Lord!</u> New York: Morehouse-Barlow, 1974.

Hynes, Arleen. <u>The Passover Meal: A Ritual for Christian Homes</u>. New York: Paulist Press, 1972.

116

Jamison, Andrew. <u>Liturgies for Children</u>. Cincinnati: St. Anthony Messenger Press, 1975.

Jeep, Elizabeth McMahon and Huck, Gabe. <u>Celebrate Summer! A Guidebook for Families</u>, and <u>Celebrate Summer! A Guidebook for Congregations</u>. New York: Paulist Press, 1973.

Landry, Carey and Kinghorn, Carol Jean. <u>Hi God!</u> Cincinnati: North American Liturgy Resurces, 1973.

LeBlanc, Etienne and Talbot, Mary Rose. <u>How Green Is Green? 38 Eucharistic Celebrations for Today's Youth</u>. Notre Dame: Ave Maria Press, 1973.

Miffleton, Jack; Blunt, Neil; Blandford, Elizabeth and Bucher, Janet Marie. <u>Come Out! Kit</u>. Cincinnati: World Library Publications, 1971.

Nickerson, Betty. <u>Celebrate the Sun</u>. Toronto: McClelland & Stewart, 1969.

<u>Parishes and Families</u>. ed. Gabe Huck & Virginia Sloyan. Washington, D.C.: The Liturgical Conference, 1976.

Pottebaum, Gerard. <u>Go In Peace; Four celebrations in preparation for penance</u>. New York: Herder & Herder, 1969.

Rabalais, Maria and Hall, Howard. <u>Children, Celebrate!</u> New York: Paulist Press, 1974.

_____; Hall, Howard and Vavasseur, Donald. <u>Come! Be Reconciled</u>. New York: Paulist Press, 1975.

<u>Repent and Believe</u>. ed. William Freburger. Baltimore: Diocese of Baltimore, 320 Cathedral St., 1971.

<u>Seven Penitential Services</u>. Chicago: Archdiocese of Chicago, Liturgy Training Program, 5947 No. Manton Avenue, 1971.

<u>Signs, Songs and Stories: Another look at children's liturgies</u>. ed. Virginia Sloyan. Washington, D.C.: The Liturgical Conference, 1974.

Tietjen, Mary Louise. <u>Alleluia Days</u>. West Mystic, Conn.: Twenty-Third Publications, 1975.

Periodicals

<u>A.I.M.</u> (Aids in Ministry). Paluch Publications, Box 367, Princeton, New Jersey 08550.

<u>Catechist</u>. 2451 East River Road, Suite 200, Dayton, Ohio 45439.

Colloquy. United Church Press, 1505 Race Street, Philadelphia, Pennsylvania 19102.

Folk Mass and Modern Liturgy. P. O. Box 444, Saratoga, California 95070.

Liturgy. The Liturgical Conference, 1220 Massachusetts Avenue, N.W., Washington, D.C. 20005.

Religion Teacher's Journal. Twenty-Third Publications, P.O. Box 180, West Mystic, Connecticut 06388.

Texts

Graded religion texts and manuals used to prepare children for their first reception of the Eucharist, or for the sacraments of confirmation or reconciliation usually contain good suggestions for prayer celebrations.

Elephants and eskimos are the sort of inventions makes
me sure that God has a couple three four kids of His own.

Kenneth Patchen

Part II:
AUDIO-VISUAL AIDS

* ** * ** * ** * ** * ** * **

Communication is a way of making love to people, or reaching them. It's a most mysterious and deeply moving experience. Love and art are two ways of communicating. That's why art is so close to love.

Leonard Bernstein

* ** * ** * ** * ** * ** * **

PREFACE

Language is a means of getting at life's meaning, but is not the substance of that meaning itself. The very nature of language, coupled with the limited experience of most people, often makes it difficult to convey ideas, transmit information, and change attitudes effectively without resources beyond the written or even spoken word.

In this electronic age of ours, audiovisual expression is an essential dimension in communication. It is especially essential to a teacher of religion for a clear, interesting, and purposive communication. Teachers must add to their communicative skills the abilities to select ready-made instructional materials or to transfer ideas into specific visual forms that help them teach more effectively. Research has proven and experience has confirmed the fact that children and also adults learn far more readily from a multi-sensory and imaginative presentation than from the teacher's voice alone.

Audiovisuals are indispensable tools of communication. But, like all good tools, they can be dulled by misuse. They are not intended as entertainment nor classroom baby-sitters nor substitutes for either a good teacher or good teaching. An audiovisual aid is used to clarify, enrich, and supplement the work of the teacher. It is not in competition with the printed word but is simply one of the many ways for a teacher to present a message. Failure to understand the real role of audiovisuals can result in underrating them or using them only as a concession to the students' lack of interest in reading a text or listening attentively to the teacher.

888-8-888-8-888-8-888-8-888-8-888-8-888-8-888-8-888-8-888-

Today in our cities most learning occurs outside of the classroom.
The sheer quantity of information conveyed by the press, mass film,
TV and radio far exceeds the quantity of information conveyed by
school instruction and texts. This challenge has destroyed the
monopoly of the book as a teaching aid and cracked the very walls
of the classroom so suddenly we were confused and baffled . . . In
this violently upsetting social situation many teachers naturally
view the offerings of the new media as entertainment rather than
education, but his view carries no conviction to the student.

Marshall McLuhan

888-8-888-8-888-8-888-8-888-8-888-8-888-8-888-8-888-8-888-

Chapter 13: FILMS

To understand our world, we need to "see" everything, everywhere, look into the past and examine the future, and, on occasion, temporarily acquire a kind of "supersight" which permits us to slow down or speed up, enlarge or diminish natural and scientific occurrences.

(Wittich and Schuller, _Audiovisual Materials_. Harper & Bros.)

Today, much of this kind of "seeing" is possible in the classroom through the use of films.

Why do "entertainment" or "secular" films belong in the religion class?

1. Films create a greater sense of reality and a more lasting impression than any other audiovisual technique.

    Research has established the fact that films increase learning. In one survey, films increased pupils' knowledge of places, personages, and events from 19 to 35%, and it stimulated 40% more free reading. But intellectual knowledge will not be much good if it fails to make an impression on the student. Good films can give the students the experience of feeling as well as of understanding. Good films not only instruct but more importantly they can also inspire. (See Wittich and Schuller, p. 355.)

2. Certain ideas can best be shown through motion.

    The opening of a flower in the springtime or the facial expression of a person caught in a difficult situation can create an immediacy and sense of "presence" which a vocal discription or even a still picture cannot always produce in children.

3. The motion picture compels attention.

    With the room darkened and the film offering the only "distraction," a student almost cannot help watching. This heightens the possibility of offering an intense experience sometimes of high emotional quality.

4. The motion picture heightens reality.

The editing, which may involve manipulation of time, space, or objects, can heighten reality by eliminating distractions and by telescoping the time element. The skillfully produced film causes the viewer to identify with the life situation on the screen. This identification means more effective communcation.

5. The motion picture can bring the distant past and the present into the classroom.

Children can be present at events or in situations of which they have had no firsthand experience.

6. The motion picture builds a common denominator of experience.

Discussion, action, or deeper insight must be built upon experience.

7. The motion picture can influence attitudes.

Research has shown that films have definite, lasting effects on the social attitudes of children and that a number of pictures pertaining to the same issue may have a cumulative effect on attitude.

8. The film can promote an understanding of abstract relationships.

Situations and relationships which are difficult to analyze in real life can be shown with greater clarity and directness in a film, and this can provide a basis for discussion and greater understanding of real life situations.

CAUTION!

The film must not be thought of as merely a mechanical device for instructing. It is an art form which is very much a part of the lives of young people. They watch movies on television as well as at their neighborhood theater and drive-in. With the vivid impact a film can make, it can be capable of imparting the spirit of religion so necessary in the lives of Christian students, which so often does not seem to be imparted to them through the conventional methods of teaching religion.

But since all films are not equally suitable for the religion classroom, and because of the great variety available, each teacher must develop both an eye for the potential uses of a film, and a sense of discrimination.

There are many "religious" films available. Some are good (Monsieur Vincent, The Passion of Joan of Arc, Inn of the Sixth Happiness), but others are of such poor artistic quality that they risk causing scorn or distaste for the message they proclaim. A poor film about a saint does an injustice both to the saint and to the God whom he or she served, and should never be shown in religion class. Lists of religious films are easy to find, and since their purpose and use is rather obvious, no further comment on them is necessary here. Producers-distributors of religious films are listed at the end of this chapter.

Two kinds of commercial films are available: full-length features (usually about 90 minutes) and shorts (10 to 60 minutes). Both can be used profitably in classes of junior and senior high school students, but full-length pictures are not recommended for use with primary and intermediate grades. Most religion classes are not long enough to show the film, and the follow-up discussion or activity would have to be delayed by a day or a week--lessening the impact of the experience. One must also consider the attention and immobility span of grade school children as well as their tendency to become involved in the details of a long movie, missing the point of the event.

There may be special occasions (such as vacation school) when a feature film can be used, or a special film may turn up that is so good that you want to arrange a longer class period in order to show it. Perhaps several days a semester could be set aside for a film and discussion for the junior high students. They would benefit not only from the film itself but also from developing the skill of film interpretation.

WHAT IS A "GOOD" CLASSROOM FILM?

It is one that: is artistically good
is a suitable length for the group
is true to the human/divine reality it portrays
is dynamically presented.

It makes an impact on the viewer.

It gives the viewer deeper insight into something real.

STEPS IN SUCCESSFUL FILM PROJECTION:

1. Selection:

Know your curriculum; have a sharply focused purpose in showing a film. Select a film according to its teaching potential, artistic merit, and relevancy for your group.

125

Order film weeks, even months in advance.

2. Preview:

Have some of the children preview it with you and help develop the preparation and conclusion.

Have some of the children preview it and act as a discussion panel after the showing.

AS YOU PREVIEW, ASK YOURSELF THESE QUESTIONS:

Does it really teach what we want to discuss?
Is its portrayal of life situations true and compelling?
How can the children be prepared to get the most from it?
Should only a portion be used?
Should it be stopped for discussion at some point?
Should it be shown without introduction?
What discussion questions will best draw out students' insights
    and opinions?
What follow-up activities does it suggest?

3. Projection Arrangements:

Test all equipment and mechanical arrangements in advance; thread projector in advance; have a competent projectionist on hand; have an extra bulb and fuse.

4. Introduction:

Introductory remarks can help explain difficult parts of a film; questions that require careful observation may increase attention. BUT with some films it is much more effective to say nothing before showing it.

In general, if the film is used for instruction, background information, discussion or concept development, you should share with your group a clearly stated purpose.

5. Film Showing:

The room should be adequately darkened and adequately ventilated, and each person should be able to see and hear without difficulty.

The teacher should stay in the room with the group even though he or she has seen the film already.

6. Follow-Up:

Discussion, activity, silence--or whatever has been planned to help the children absorb and understand the meaning of the film.

Many teachers start the discussion with the question, "What is this film about?" After the objective reporting of what the film portrayed, the teacher may ask, "What do you think the director (writer, actors) tried to tell us?" Finally the question, "What did you feel; how did you respond to the movie?" may be asked. The teacher will be amazed at the different opinions expressed by the students. The better the film, the more insights the students will receive. The teacher must carry on the discussion in an organized fashion, by leading from one question to the next--always LISTENING to the students rather than over-explaining or preaching. Questions should never be phrased in such a way that a simple "yes" or "no" will suffice.

TECHNICAL TIPS:

1. Projector:

   All equipment should be in good mechanical condition. A faulty projector can cause expensive damage to films. Projector noise can be very distracting; therefore, if possible, project from an adjoining room or from a balcony. It may be possible to construct a projection room if films are shown frequently in the church "theater." If the projector cannot be separated in this way it should be elevated so that it is not necessary to create an aisle down the middle. In any case, equipment should be as inconspicuous as possible with wiring put where people will not trip on it.

   The projector bulb should be strong enough for the size picture which must be shown, usually 750-1000 watts.

2. Sound:

   In projecting 16mm film only half as much footage goes around the sound drum as in the case of 35mm theatrical film. Therefore, 16mm sound is inherently somewhat inferior. It is recommended, then, that two speakers be used, one on either side, put at approximately ear level. Speakers from other projectors may be used if their plug-ins are similar. A good used speaker may be bought for about $25. Volume should be checked at various points throughout the room, and during projection constant attention should be paid to the volume control.

3. Screen:

   A beaded or silver screen should be used. Projection to more than 100 people will usually call for a larger-than-average screen.

4. Seating:

From the center of the screen any theater extends in a 180 degree arc. However, it is from the central 30 degree segment that the brightest and truest image is seen. There is always a degree of dullness and distortion on either side.

5. Ventilation:

An average body gives off as much heat as does a 100 watt light bulb. Therefore, it is important that the room have adequate, draft-free ventilation.

6. Music:

It is best if early arrivals do not enter a "cold" room to wait in uneasy silence for things to start. Recorded music may be played through the projector speaker system both before the film and during reel changes. Rehearsal of such technical business is highly recommended.

7. Projecting:

The first reel should be set in advance so that the first image on the screen is the beginning film title. When beginning a new reel, hold a hand in front of the projector until the opening frames ap-

pear. Never project the countdown leader; at the end of the reel
turn off the projector lamp so that the bright screen is not shown.
Also turn down the sound at this time.

The sound must be turned on about 10 seconds before projecting so
that the sound system is warmed up. If the sound is fuzzy, the
film loop is probably not passing tightly enough around the sound
drum and must be rethreaded at this point.

If dust shows up at the edge of the picture you may blow it out
of the projector gate either from the top in some projectors or
by using a syringe with others.

If the loop is lost, experienced projectionists will know what to
do. It is seldom necessary to turn on the lights for this purpose.

It is best to rewind the film and pack up the equipment only after
everyone has left the room if there are discussions which might be
disturbed.

IMPORTANT ANNOUNCEMENT:

IF YOU CAN'T FIND A FILM JUST RIGHT FOR YOUR STUDENTS, WHY NOT MAKE ONE!

If your students are teenagers, let them do the job; if they are young,
ask some teenagers to help you make it.

For some suggestions on film-making, see Chapter 10.

The average 18-year-old has seen 500 feature films, and
15,000 hours of television, but
has spent only 10,800 hours of total school time from kindergarten
through high school.
Only sleep time surpasses television-viewing time as a prime activity.
Among the college-age group, the ratio of films to novels is 20 to 1.

(From a survey by Rev. J. M. Culkin, Director, Center of
Communications, Fordham University)

Earlier editions of this book included lists of free and rental films which can be used to good advantage in religious education programs and in celebrations and prayer services. The last few years have witnessed such a "media explosion" that it is no longer possible to list even the best of such films. Excellent catalogues and newsletters are now available to serve this purpose. Short Films in Religious Education by William Kuhns (CEBCO/Pflaum, 1967) with its supplement, and Mass Media, the bi-weekly newsletter of Mass Media Ministries (2116 North Charles Street, Baltimore, Maryland 21218) are especially excellent. Also consult: William Kuhns' book, Exploring the Film (CEBCO/Pflaum, 1968), the November, 1966 issue of Motive magazine, and A Guide to Short Films for Religious Education Programs by Patrick J. McCaffery (Fides, 1967).

A good religion teachers' library should also include catalogues from the film producers and distributors listed below, as well as information from the public library media center, the public school curriculum library, the diocesan or regional religious education media center, and a clipping file for reviews and articles on the subject.

For a catalogue of free films, at a moderate cost, write to: Educators Program Service, Randolph, Wisconsin 53956. Ask for their Educators' Guide to Free Films, and Educators' Guide to Social Studies Free Materials.

PRODUCERS/DISTRIBUTORS OF FILMS

American Documentary Films
    336 West 84th Street, New York, N.Y. 10024

Argus Communications
    3505 North Ashland Avenue, Chicago, Illinois 60657

Association Films, Inc.
    1621 Dragon Street, Dallas, Texas 75207

Audio Film Classics
    2138 East 75th Street, Chicago, Illinois 60649

Brandon Films, Inc.
    % Film Center, Inc., 20 East Huron Street, Chicago, Illinois 60611

Cathedral Films, Inc.
    2921 West Alameda Avenue, Burbank, California 91505

Concordia Films
    3558 South Jefferson Avenue, St. Louis, Missouri 63118

Contemporary Films/McGraw-Hill
    1221 Avenue of the Americas, New York, N.Y. 10020

Continental 16
    241 East 34th Street, New York, N.Y. 10016

Don Bosco Films
    New Rochelle, New York 10802

Feature Film Directory (catalogue available of all films)
    250 West 57th Street, New York, N.Y. 10019

Films Incorporated (subsidiary of Encyclopedia Britannica)
    1414 Dragon Street, Dallas, Texas 75207

Franciscan Communications Center (Teleketics)
    1229 South Santee Street, Los Angeles, California 90015

Ideal Film
    1611 Boston Street, Tulsa, Oklahoma 74114

Ikonographics, Inc.
    P.O. Box 4454, Louisville, Kentucky 40204

LaSalle Catechetical Center
    3501 Solly Avenue, Philadelphia, Pennsylvania 19136

Learning Corporation of America (Searching for Values)
    711 Fifth Avenue, New York, New York 10022

Mass Media Ministries
    2116 North Charles Street, Baltimore, Maryland 21218

Museum of Modern Art Film Library
    11 West 53rd Street, New York, N.Y. 10019

National Audio-Visual Association, Inc.
    3150 Spring Street, Fairfax, Virginia 22030

NCCM Film Center
    405 Lexington Avenue, New York, New York 10017

ROA Films
    1696 North Astor Street, Milwaukee, Wisconsin 53202

Sterling Educational Films
    P.O. Box 8497, Universal City, Los Angeles, California 91608

University of Southern California (USC)
    Film Distribution Service, University Park, Los Angeles, California 90007

WBBM-TV Film Loan Library
    630 North McClur Court, Chicago, Illinois 60611

        We find ourselves in the presence of a work of
art when the actors, actions, and objects of the foreground appear
transparent and lead our glance to the basic themes of human existence.

                                              Rudolf Arnheim

Chapter 14: FILMSTRIPS

Filmstrips are a popular and relatively inexpensive form of audio-visual communication. A filmstrip consists of a series of still photographs prepared for projection on a 35mm film. Frequently a phonograph record with narration for each frame will accompany the filmstrip. A printed copy of that narration is usually provided so that the filmstrip and record can be coordinated, or so that the teacher may give the narration instead of using the record.

Because filmstrips can be shown as slowly as a teacher wishes, they are especially adaptable to young children. There is no age limit to their use, however, and some of the most excellent religious filmstrips available today are designed for an adult audience.

FILMSTRIPS ARE EASY TO USE:

*The pictures are in a pre-set sequence, so that they will not get out of order (as slides or individual pictures might).

*Both filmstrip and projector are easy to carry, so that teachers can take them home for previewing and lesson preparation.

*The projector is easy to operate.

*The filmstrip comes in a small container which is easy to file and store.

FILMSTRIPS ARE VERSATILE:

*A picture can be left on the screen for any length of time, for study or discussion.

*The strip can easily be turned back to review a scene.

*The filmstrip can be used in a large auditorium filled with people, in a small classroom, or by an individual student at a browsing table (a piece of white cardboard acting as a screen).

FILMSTRIPS ARE REASONABLY PRICED (usually!)

Because of the pre-set sequence of the filmstrip, when one or two frames become outdated by changes going on in the Church the whole strip becomes useless. If it is only the narration, however, and not the picture which becomes out-of-date, it is possible to write a new script, and read it yourself during the filming.

GUIDELINES FOR EFFECTIVE USE OF FILMSTRIPS are basically the same as those governing any other audio-visual aid:

1. PREVIEW THE FILMSTRIP:

Is it suitable for the age and maturity of my students? What is its artistic quality? (There are many "religious" filmstrips available that have extremely poor art, so the teacher should be wary--poor taste can undermine a fine script and deft manipulation of the projector.)

2. FIT THE FILMSTRIP INTO THE LEARNING PATTERN OF YOUR CLASS:

What do I want to communicate by means of this visual aid? Is this strip merely entertaining or is it a catalyst in the learning process? Does this strip rely on my enthusiasm for the subject, or does it have some ability to hold the students' interest, and will it awaken their enthusiasm?

3. PREPARE THE PRESENTATION:

Does this strip introduce a new topic? furnish new information? summarize a unit? What kind of presentation will best accomplish this purpose --a panel, a forum, a discussion, part of a ceremony of worship? Shall I introduce it, or should a student or a committee of students introduce it? Should all of it be shown or only a certain part? Are there special scenes, themes, and so forth to which I should draw the children's attention?

4. ATTEND TO THE TECHNICAL DETAILS:

Does it have a record or reading script? Who will read? Who will project it? Have I practiced running the projector and synchronizing the filmstrip with the record? Do I have all the necessary equipment on hand (including an extension cord, record player if there is a record, extra bulb for the projector)? Can all the students hear? see?

5. <u>FOLLOW UP THE SHOWING IN ORDER TO DEEPEN THE LEARNING</u>:

What will I do immediately following the presentation? later? Do I have definite questions in mind to increase the children's understanding of what they have seen? How can I make it possible for them to express their personal reactions to the filmstrip? To what extent can this filmstrip be used to teach related matters?

<u>SOME SUGGESTIONS FOR CREATIVE USE OF FILMSTRIPS</u>:

<u>Multiple showing</u>. Tell the children that they will see the filmstrip twice, and that they will have a chance to talk about the pictures. The first time they see the filmstrip they are to listen, but the second time they will explain the pictures in their own words. This puts the children on the alert, and makes them more attentive. Show the strip using the prepared record or script, or explaining it with your own words. The second time the strip is shown (immediately or some time later) let the children talk. Ask them questions; let them explain what they think they see in the pictures; let them put it in their own words.

<u>Partial Showing</u>. At times you will want to use the portion of a strip that pertains to the topic of your lesson, although the strip as a whole emphasizes a different theme. In the filmstrip <u>The Father's Love</u> (reel 2 of the series <u>Parables of the Kingdom</u>, Roa Films), for instance, it is possible to end the showing with the feast which the father orders to celebrate the return of his prodigal son. By thus eliminating the episode of the jealous older brother, you can concentrate the children's attention on the love and forgiveness of the father and on the sorrowful confession and return of the son. This is especially helpful for younger children who are easily distracted by more than one plot in a story.

<u>Single Frame</u>. One frame can be used for a discussion starter, the background for a story or a reading from the Bible, the backdrop for a drama, or a focus of meditation in a worship ceremony or time of quiet prayer. During a unit of study on prayer, for instance, a filmstrip portraying the interview between Moses and God at the burning bush can be shown to bring out the reverence Moses paid to God by removing his shoes and bowing down to Him (episode 2 of <u>Moses and the Covenant</u>, Roa Films). It can also illustrate the fact that in prayer Moses received a message that caused him to direct his life in a certain way. As a climax to the entire unit, which may have lasted for several lessons, or several weeks, the frame of Moses kneeling before God can be shown, and the children asked to think in silence of <u>their</u> relationship to God in prayer.

<u>Multiple Use</u>. The same filmstrip can often be used for many different purposes. Your introductory remarks as well as the script or preparation will direct the students' attention toward a certain theme. Sometimes a new script can be written in order to shift the emphasis somewhat. The same strip should not be used over and over again with the same group of children, however. Neither should it be used year after year for the same

group. Filmstrips showing the crossing of the Red Sea by the Israelites
(episode 4, frame 10, Moses and the Covenant) and their eating of the manna
(episode 4, frame 26) could be shown in connection with lessons on baptism
and the Eucharist, respectively.

The background material for the teacher, which is included in most sets
of filmstrips, will often point out some additional uses of the strips.

PRODUCERS/DISTRIBUTORS OF FILMSTRIPS

Concordia Publishing Co.
   3558 South Jefferson Avenue, St. Louis, Missouri 63118

Don Bosco Filmstrips
   New Rochelle, New York 10802

Family Filmstrips
   5823 Santa Monica Boulevard, Hollywood, California 90038

Ikonographics, Inc.
   P.O. Box 4454, Louisville, Kentucky 40204

John & Mary Harrell
   Box 9006, Berkeley, California 97409

Morehouse-Barlow Co.
   78 Danbury Road, Wilton, Connecticut 06897

Pflaum/Standard
   8121 Hamilton Avenue, Cincinnati, Ohio 45231

Roa Films
   1696 North Astor Street, Milwaukee, Wisconsin 53202

Synesthetics, Inc.
   Box 254, Cos Cob, Connecticut 06807

Teleketics/Franciscan Communications Center
   1229 South Santee Street, Los Angeles, California 90015

Thomas S. Klise
   P.O. Box 3418, Peoria, Illinois 61614

Twenty-Third Publications
   P.O. Box 180, West Mystic, Connecticut 06388

Weston Woods Studios, Inc.
   Weston, Connecticut 06880

Chapter 15: STILL PICTURES

Pictures, a universal and indispensable teaching tool, have always been used by good teachers to arouse interest, stimulate discussion, raise questions, supply information and ideas, point out relationships, and otherwise contribute to learning. Pictures can overcome barriers of time and distance, bringing historical scenes (Anne Frank's house) and far places (Vietnam), and famous people (John F. Kennedy) into the classroom. They can enlarge or reduce scenes otherwise unseen by the naked eye (the world seen from Apollo 9), they can focus attention on some aspect of everyday life that is ordinarily taken for granted (see The Family of Man), and they can capture emotions that words are unable to describe. Pictures can be shown singly or in groups, in black and white or in color, printed on paper or projected on a wall, still or with an illusion of motion.

Today the resources from which a teacher can find "flat" or "still" photographs, slides, drawings, and reproductions of fine art are almost unlimited and extremely reasonable in cost. Teachers in poor parishes, even "non-professional" Sunday school teachers have developed excellent picture files, using illustrations taken from back issues of Life, Look, National Geographic, Ebony, and Witness, and from carefully chosen commercial sets of "religious" pictures. Such a file is a valuable resource for all teachers regardless of other materials that are available to them. A file of slides is also very useful.

To be effective, pictures must be understood, and not everyone is able to "read" pictures in exactly the same way. A young child develops first the ability to identify the shapes and lines on a paper as representing familiar objects. Then is developed the ability to describe the objects which are seen. Finally, the child becomes able to interpret and draw inferences--in other words, able to realize that the picture implies a story. To observe the three steps of development, a teacher can ask children aged 5, 7, and 9 to look at a given picture and describe what they see. Their answers should illustrate the three levels of maturity.

Psychologists have discovered that in looking at a picture, the normal person's eyes fall immediately on the center of interest and then move rapidly over the whole picture. This initial survey is followed by a closer examination of details, apparently with more personal response and interpretation. It is important, then, to allow enough viewing time for the child to see the picture thoroughly and absorb it. Directions given to persons before they look at a picture appear to have a direct bearing on the amount of involvement and observation they give to the picture. This direction can be given with questions, tactfully worded statements, conversation. It would be a shame, however, to over-explain the content of a picture so that the visual aspect of the experience is robbed of its effectiveness.

Even though pictures are in a sense a universal language, there are extensive individual differences in "picture seeing." Obviously the observer's perception is conditioned by past experience with picture-reading as well as by social, educational, and cultural environment. Although most of the children we meet in our classrooms have a rich background of picture-books which parents read to them, and movies and TV shows that they have shared with their family and perhaps heard discussed, there are some groups of children who lack these experiences. Therefore they require more guidance in drawing benefit from a visual experience in the classroom.

> It is literally true that we can not have a better world than we can picture. We can improve our schools, our homes, the work of our legislative bodies only as we can develop certain images in the minds of people-- and pictures can create such images.
>
> Dryden

SELECTING PICTURES

The visual images which we offer children in their religion classes will have a permanent influence upon their conceptualization and reaction to God, the Church, and religious matters. Visual images do not merely illustrate. They teach. It is essential, therefore, that sufficient thought be given to a discriminating selection of pictures and other visual aids. There are no clear-cut, easily applied rules for this selection--it must depend upon the religious insight and good taste of the teacher as well as sensitivity to the maturity and background of the students. In general the teacher will judge a picture according to the SIMPLICITY, STRENGTH, AND DYNAMISM OF THE IMAGE, the TRUTH OF ITS PORTRAYAL OF LIFE, its RELEVANCE TO THE LIVES OF THE STUDENTS, and its SUITABILITY TO THE CLASSROOM SITUATION.

The younger the children, the simpler the picture must be both in detail and in the idea conveyed. Home and family scenes taken from magazines should bear some resemblance to the milieu of the students unless the picture portrays people of a different background for a specific purpose.

In choosing pictures one may use religious or catechetical pictures, reproductions of fine art (both religious and "secular" themes), and magazine pictures. Caution should be exercised in the selection of religious visual aids, however, as many are of inferior artistic quality. A picture of a biblical event should try to portray more than the physical appearance of the scene.

138

> The picture that simply records historical facts
> reproduces the incident "as it could have been" and
> not "how it is." Such a picture degrades the Gospel
> to merely a historical report . . . . It fails to give
> those events of the past a meaning here and now.
> What has a picture of the gale on Lake Genezareth to
> tell here and now? What does a picture of Christ
> raising Lazarus from the dead have to tell us here and
> now? This is the challenge of the artist.
>
> Gerard A. Pottebaum

In the portrayal of Christ, especially, the artist must convey something
of the Messiah of faith, as well as the Jesus of history--and above all,
the image of Christ should be strong, masculine, and truly human, rather
than weak, feminine, and sentimentally "pretty." It is better not to use
any picture at all than to use one that leaves a false impression such as
that of an effeminate Christ.

Well-defined and specific objectives are particularly helpful in select-
ing pictures. In a lesson on "new life" for Easter, for example, a picture
of a young colt with its mother can be very effective. If it shows a stormy
sky, however, and all of the horses are racing to the barn, the picture
should be discarded because the storm and the fear of the animals will be
more absorbing to the children than the newness and joy-in-living of the
little colt. Wittich and Schuler quote an intermediate grade teacher who
said: "I had used pictures for more years than I care to admit before it
dawned on me that my best lessons with pictures were those lessons where I
had the clearest idea of what I wanted each picture to do for the class."

It is also a good rule to use as few pictures as possible in order to
convey a concept vividly. Never use two pictures if one will accomplish
your task.

A strong photograph will illustrate any good set of words or ideas, but
a weak photograph will always tend to obscure and deaden a meaning. In
Let's See, No. 1 by Celia Hubbard (Paulist/Newman), there are some fine
suggestions for improving one's powers of discrimination. Find four pic-

tures that you think are effective, for example. Pin them to the wall, and after a week replace the one you like least with a better one. Or, take an issue of Life or Look; tear out each photograph and advertisement; divide them into piles that you like and don't like.

PUTTING PICTURES TO WORK

Pictures can:

> translate word symbols: "savior," "Easter vigil"

> enrich or substitute for reading: "modern Israel"

> introduce a story or topic, by providing an
> immediate, unspoken orientation: photographs
> of A Man for All Seasons.

A skillful teacher integrates the picture into the lesson. Perhaps it is shown at the beginning of class, and the children are led to look and think through the teacher's questions and comments. At other times the picture is best presented at the middle of the lesson, or perhaps at the end, when the children are asked to look at it in silence. Father Josef Goldbrunner, the German catechist, likes to hold a picture up, and, without a word, draw the children's eyes and attention to various things in the picture by simply pointing to them slowly.

Often the picture used in a lesson can be posted on a bulletin board, perhaps with a caption and/or one or two other pictures. A picture of two mothers at the graveside of their children in Aberfan, Wales (Life, December, 1966), can be posted with the words ". . . and the angel said to the women, "Why do you look for the living among the dead?" On bulletin boards as well as in a lesson, it is more effective to use FEW pictures, not many.

In planning lessons, do not forget to make good use of the teaching potential of the pictures in the children's text--if they are good.

MAGAZINE CANDIDS

It is impossible to "teach religion" these days without a stack of picture magazines. The juxtaposing of contemporary photographs and advertisements with the Gospel message is one of the best ways of communicating the relevance of the Gospel to modern life, the contemporary equivalent of the biblical symbols, and the many faces of the Christ who lives today among us. Unless Christians learn to see and hear Christ in current events, they won't see and hear Christ in biblical events.

Photography is the vernacular of the arts because everyone can understand something of what is being communicated. Its use in religion class can . . .

> . . . help students make connections between visible and invisible realities,
>
> . . . help students discover and create new symbols,
>
> . . . help students look at something and see something deeper,
>
> . . . help students understand the newest medium of the art of our times.

The magazine candid is a teaching method which tries to convey just that. A series of magazine photographs are chosen which illustrate a scriptural passage or theme. They are then shown (usually with the aid of an opaque projector) while a narrator reads from the Bible or from a script composed for the presentation. Music which fits the mood of the presentation should be played also. The script and picture combination is something like a film-strip, though it is more flexible and uses contemporary pictures instead of art work. A magazine candid can be developed and presented either by the teacher or by the students. In the process of creating a magazine candid, the students have to think about the real meaning of the topic and its translation into modern visual terms. They have to look over many pictures, and exercise judgment and discrimination in choosing the ones they want to use.

The magazine candid can be simple or complex. Part of a unit on brotherhood, for example, can be a study of racial tensions and efforts toward racial understanding. Pictures can be gathered from various magazines and newspapers, and the teacher can simply comment on each one as it is shown. A more elaborate presentation might include a narration prepared in advance, taped newsreports of race riots and interviews with defenders of opposing points of view, and some "soul music."

The commentary and musical background can be taped. The pictures and script can be filed and used again. Mounted properly the pictures will last indefinitely; marked properly (for example, 'Prod. Son, pic. 8') they can be used at other times and then reassembled in sequence. If there will be no need to separate the pictures again, the magazine candid can be mounted on a single strip of shelf paper. This facilitates rolling it through the opaque projector and will keep it in order for the presentation.

PROJECTED PRESENTATION--A WORD OF CAUTION

When a room is darkened to begin the lesson, a psychological change is introduced to the classroom atmosphere that makes special demands upon the teacher. Projection is dramatic; students are led to expect something out of the ordinary. When you project a motion picture, the device itself does most of the performing, but when using still pictures you yourself must assume the major burden.

The performance must be well planned in all respects. Every student must see and hear clearly; the materials to be projected must be readily at hand and properly arranged; mechanics must be under control. This does not mean, of course, that you must do a superb job of showmanship in which you do all the talking. It means rather that you must be completely prepared with questions, comments, and explanations. The projected lesson, in short, calls for thorough preparation as opposed to off-the-cuff improvisation.

The opaque projector can project pictures in books such as small maps or pictures that could not otherwise be shared by the whole class at the same time. It will even project small objects. When showing a magazine candid, change the pictures slowly and smoothly. The viewer must have the time to absorb each picture, and not be distracted by too much fumbling.

STARTING A COLLECTION

Teachers seldom have the time (or money!) to mount their pictures until just before using them in class. This is not a problem unless there are so many people using the file that the pictures get damaged. Special articles (for example, the Life articles on Greece) can be stapled together and put in a separate file, or given a booklet type of cover.

Large filing envelopes can be made from Kraft paper, folded in half, and stapled, or fastened at the sides with masking tape. A piece of heavy cardboard inside will make them more durable. The "file" could be an ordinary corrugated box. Be sure to get rid of the poor pictures! You will begin to do this automatically as your file thickens and your experience grows.

A slide file can be developed at a moderate cost. Commercial slides are available on religious themes (for example, the Holy Land), on historic places, scientific subjects, or your home town (check your local drugstore or souvenir counter). Friends or fellow parishioners may have some slides suitable for a presentation that you are putting together on "family life" or "water" or "nature"--shots from vacation trips, etc.

You can have a slide made from any good magazine picture.

One of the best ways to develop a set of slides is to take your camera and do-it-yourself. This is an excellent project for students because they can look at a place differently when they go there with a camera in hand. They could be asked, for example, to make a set of slides that portray the feeling of their school, or the downtown area of their town.

FILING YOUR COLLECTION

Here is a suggested list of topics which might be used for file headings. More may be added as need arises. It is a good idea to mark pictures for easy refiling.

142

nature-beautiful; nature-powerful.
animals; insects; birds
babies and children
teenagers
adults; careers
families and home
food; clothing
communication; transportation; recreation
art and architecture
religious; old testament; new testament; church
    figures
poverty; disease
war; riots
tragedy and disaster; race problems
the city; the nation; the world.

A LAST WORD ABOUT PICTURES--and other visual aids: Use something else
if you can find something that is better. For example, pictures about
spring and new life cannot have the same impact as a trip to the schoolyard
to look at the new blades of grass and buds on the trees, or the actual
hatching of some baby chicks, or a butterfly in the classroom.

EVERYTHING FORMS US--THE MOUNTAINS, OCEANS, FLOWERS, OUTER SPACE,
            THE SPIDER'S WEB--

    ALL THESE THINGS FORM US, IF WE TAKE THE TIME TO LOOK AT THEM.

BECAUSE THEY GIVE US A SENSE OF WONDER--WHICH IS A PREAMBLE TO WORSHIP--
            THEY FORM US.

                                        Stanley Grabowski

PRODUCERS/DISTRIBUTORS OF SLIDE PRESENTATIONS

(a series of slides on a theme, with or
without a script)

Camelot Communciations ("I'm A People")
    Minneapolis, Minnesota

Mark IV Presentations
    La Salette Center, Attleboro, Massachusetts 02703

New Life Films ("Visual & Verbal Meditations")
    Box 2008, Kansas City, Kansas 66110

Paulist Press ("Discovery in Sight," "Images and Explorations," "Imagepaks,"
    "Paulist Paks," "Probing the World")
    400 Sette Drive, Paramus, New Jersey 07652

Saint Mary's College Press ("The Slide Library")
    Winona, Minnesota 55987

Society for Visual Education, Inc. ("Slideas")
    1345 Diversey Parkway, Chicago, Illinois 60614
    Order from: Loyola University Press
            3441 North Ashland Avenue, Chicago, Illinois 60657

Chapter 16: TAPE RECORDINGS

Today's world has become so accustomed to written and printed words that a classroom experience of "pure listening" may seem dull or unnecessary. It is important to remember, however, that half of the adult population of the world can neither read nor write. But they can listen understandingly. Though incapable of interpreting the symbols of a printed page, they manage effectively with spoken symbols only. Reading is a fairly new skill for most of the people on this earth. Throughout centuries the human race conserved its great stories and wisdom solely through speaking and listening; for centuries teaching was basically a matter of oral communication.

Technical inventions made possible our widespread use of printed materials at a time when the spoken word could not travel beyond the range of the speaker's voice. Today, through the application of electronics, the possibilities for oral communication have become extremely important to the teacher who must use both written and spoken symbols wisely. Both reading and listening have unique teaching values which should be exploited.

The Judeo-Christian tradition is based upon a religion of revelation-- the Word of God, spoken to men through the events of their lives. This revelation is preserved and communicated to succeeding generations through the Scriptures. A Christian is one who has heard and accepted this word--and, as St. Paul says, "How can they believe if they have not heard?" Part of the task of the religious educator, then, is to help the student develop the capacity to listen--to listen to the Word of Scripture, to the Word of the teacher and the preacher, and to the Word spoken to him personally by the Holy Spirit.

The tape recorder can be a valuable tool in providing opportunities for learning to listen. There are many other values which it offers the imaginative teacher at the same time, for it can:

> provide experience both of listening to others as they
> express their ideas and of exchanging spoken
> ideas with others, clearly and with confidence;

> provide a comparison (with others, or with myself at a
> later time);

> provide information;

> prepare a class for discussion of important issues;

> provide experiences which are so lifelike that they give the
> learner true understandings of people, places, and
> things throughout the world.

SOME SUGGESTED USES OF A TAPE RECORDER:

1. <u>MUSIC</u>

*Songs recorded by older children, talented friends, or the parish choir
   can be used to teach new songs to children. Songs may be collected
   from hymnals, records, and religion texts.

   For a training tape, have the first verse sung twice without harmony,
   then the melody alone (guitar, piano, etc.), then the whole song can
   be sung with all the flourishes. This saves a great deal of rewinding as you teach.

*Songs may be recorded from records, so that they may be stopped at inter-
   vals for discussions. Many records by the Beatles, Bob Dylan, Joan
   Baez, and so forth are valuable discussion material for junior or
   senior high school classes. Some of the popular folksongs and freedom songs are truly religious and far more authentic than many of
   the hymns we are accustomed to, while others typify the hedonism or
   alienation of our age.

*Instrumental music may be used as background for a picture presenta-
   tion or magazine candid presentation. It can be used as part of a
   Bible vigil or prayer service, or as part of an art response to the
   lesson. For example, after speaking of the wonder of God's creative
   power, you can describe the Grand Canyon; then play the <u>Grand Canyon
   Suite</u>. Instruct children just to <u>listen</u> quietly to the music once;
   then replay the music and have the children paint on large sheets of
   paper the colors or feelings that the music awakened in them. Do
   not show pictures of the Grand Canyon or encourage realistic drawing;
   the point is to share the <u>feeling of the music</u>, joining the composer
   in his celebration of God's beauty and power.

*Selections of music from different nations may be used to illustrate
the differences and likenesses among the people of God. Selections
of conversation from a foreign language tape could serve the same
purpose.

2. CONVERSATION AND DISCUSSION

*Tapes of the students' opinions, feelings, reports, or discussions can
be played for parents, other grades, the pastor. Parents would find
a third grade's discussion of conscience interesting, for example,
and the same tape might serve as a starter for discussion in a
seventh-grade class.

*Tapes of the parents' opinions or discussion on topics like "The Teen-
ager and Freedom," or "The Laity in the Church," may be used for
discussion in junior or senior high classes.

*A student's report (for example, "The Holy Land Today") can be taped
for presentation to another class, or for another year, or for further discussion at a later time.

*Interviews with local citizens who cannot come in person to talk to
the class can be useful. The police chief or juvenile judge could
talk about causes of delinquency, a social worker about life in the
slums, and the pastor about the meaning of the Eucharist. The bish-
op's words on the Holy Spirit in the Church today could be played
to children preparing for their Confirmation.

*A lesson on the Word of God can be introduced by a tape of short mes-
sages: "this is Father Smith's word--listen . . . now listen to
Mrs. Jones' word to you . . .; Sister Mary has a word for you on this
tape, too . . .; now here is another word spoken to you--listen . . .
(Scripture; reading)."

*When guests do come to speak, their lecture can be taped for future
reference and discussion.

*Sections of dialogue from movies or TV programs may be taped for dis-
cussion. In On the Waterfront the conversation in the tavern in
which Terry tells Edie his philosophy of life (get what you can and
don't become involved in other people's problems) could initiate discussion on values and life-goals.

3. NEWS BROADCASTS AND SPEECHES

*Radio and TV "specials," important speeches, debates, even commercials
can be useful in the religion lesson. By juxtaposing the Bible and
the newspaper, doctrine and daily life, the teacher creates a "living
textbook" from which the child will be able to learn long after "Sunday school" has been outgrown.

*Famous speeches can be bought from tape and record companies. Winston Churchill's "Britain's finest hour" or "Blood, Sweat, and Tears" speeches could be part of a unit on courage or leadership. Pope Paul VI's speech to the United Nations is suitable for discussion or as part of a prayer service on peace.

4. SCRIPTURAL AND LITURGICAL READINGS

   *These can be used as part of a Bible service, as part of a magazine candid, or simply to vary your usual presentation of the scriptural text for the day. The children can dramatize or pantomime the scriptural event or parable.

5. SOUNDS

   *Sounds from nature, people's voices, or mechanical devices can help to make a presentation more vivid. A tape on water, for instance (splashing, pouring into a glass, washing hands, washing up on shore or rocks, slapping side of boat, children playing in water, baby enjoying a bath, rain on roof, storm), adds an experience and an atmosphere which can lead into discussion of water as the symbol of life, grace, and baptism. Pictures could be coordinated with the sounds, making a magazine candid presentation.

   *Tapes can be made of happy sounds, sad sounds, sounds of death, springtime, the city. A tape on household sounds can be part of a lesson for young children on home as a sign of God's providence and love. These tapes draw children's attention to and deepen their appreciation of the ordinary realities of life as well as their power of hearing.

6. THE CHILD'S TEXT

   *This can be helpful to the slow reader, a class of mixed ages, a shut-in, or simply for adding variety to your presentation.

7. STORIES, POEMS, CHORAL READINGS

   *Children may pantomime, dramatize, or join in as the tape is played.

HANDLING THE MEDIUM:

The tape-recorder is a versatile teaching tool. It provides instant replay of conversation or lectures. Tapes can be erased and reused, are inexpensive and easy to store, and can be used a little at a time. A whole year's work could be recorded on one or two reels. A reel of songs can be added to at any time. Tapes can be edited and spliced. Battery-driven machines can be used for taping sounds out of doors or in a large auditorium or church where electrical outlets are not available.

The operator's manual which comes with your machine usually gives enough recording hints for the amateur. With a little experience you will become adept at placing the microphone, finding the best recording level and tone, avoiding background noise and echo, and so forth.

Before playing a tape, prepare the children to listen--help them to focus their attention by asking them to listen for certain information, ideas, or sounds. After playing the tape and discussing it, it is often good to play it again, so that they have a chance to notice some of the things they missed. Always plan to follow up the listening experience with discussion, creative art, dramatization, or some other activity which will draw upon their personal reaction to the tape.

Pre-recorded education tapes are available from National Tape Repository, National Education Association, Washington, D.C.; tapes for teaching are available through the public school system.

Chapter 17: BOOKS

Good literature presents the thoughtful reader with a point of view, an insight into life, an opinion, a philosophy. Even good children's books are intended not merely for bed-time entertainment but for the deepening and broadening of the child's awareness of reality. Since the religion class has a similar goal, it would seem that children's books can provide a rich fund of material useful in all religious education.

This is, in fact, quite true. Whether they are used to supplement the religion text or to replace it for a given unit, children's books can add a zest and creativity to the normal class.

Books, too, often have more impact in getting a point across than a text because they can be more subtle and imaginative. Texts must be clear, definite, concise, on the reading level of the student, relevant to children of all cultural, social, and emotional backgrounds. That sort of assignment reduces the chances of ever achieving true literary quality in a textbook.

There is also value in drawing children into the habit of seeing the Christian themes in "secular" books. Just as nothing can supply opportunities for discussing the religious aspects of life as generously as life itself, so good literature which reflects life accurately and vividly also stimulates some response to it.

Every teacher who has seen the "Oh, that again" look on the students' faces when "Christian fellowship" or "salvation," or "grace" is mentioned will appreciate the need for subtlety in presenting material for the children's consideration. The words of a Catholic mother, Margery Frisbie, quoted in Good Tidings (September-October 1966) have some relevance for all religious educators:

> "Some years ago, when I was eager as a novice
> to teach my children religion, a friend asked
> me, 'Don't you read your children anything but
> religious books?' I did, of course, but not
> to the extent I do now. When I gave over
> preaching myself, I made a clean sweep and
> gave up preachy authors. This cut out some
> so-called religious writers, but I've extended
> my horizons to include any author who speaks
> truly and beautifully."

THE BEST LESSONS ARE NOT NECESSARILY FOUND IN TEXTBOOKS

The best lessons are generally those which spring from something that strikes us and the children as especially meaningful. The following paragraphs describe just such a unit, taught by Mrs. Marian Stewart of Oklahome City to her fifth-grade CCD students. This unit was described in the May, 1966 issue of the bulletin of the Religious Education Office, and is reprinted here to give the reader some idea of the type of lesson which can be developed from a children's book. It is not meant to be a model for all such lessons, but as an example of how to stimulate creative thinking. Mrs. Stewart's lesson description is followed by a list of books that may be of help in the religion class.

"The Best Way To Have A Friend Is To Be A Friend"

It all started with a Christmas gift. I was given The Little Prince, by Antoine de Saint-Exupery, and I decided to share it with my fifth-grade students.

It is not a long story, and seemingly simple. Yet it touches upon many "matters of consequence." In the story, the search for a friend is a vitally important matter for the little prince. I hoped the children would understand his plight, his stubborn probing, and his discovery of the real meaning of friendship.

As we traveled with him from planet to planet we, too, began to ask many questions: who is a friend? for what reason do I choose a friend? for what qualities am I looking in a friend? do I know how to be a friend? --or am I like the little prince who said, ". . . but I was too young to know how to love my friend (the flower)."

Fifth graders are beginning to have very definite ideas about friends, and our discussion centered around the theme: the best way to have a friend is to be a friend. After looking at the list of qualities which we hoped to find in a friend, and which he, in turn, might expect of us (e.g. understanding, sincerity, the ability to share, kindness, trustworthiness, etc.), we returned to the little prince. To use a flower as a symbol for his friend seemed natural. A flower is beautiful, whole, healthy, unique; it grows; it depends on constant care.

On the flannel board we created a flower, each part representing a quality (e.g. blossom--understanding, stamen--sincerity, stem--ability to share, leaves--kindness, trustworthiness, etc.). If we removed one or the other part it was evident that our flower was not as beautiful, whole or healthy as before--something was missing.

By the same token, if we wanted to enjoy our flower (friend), we would have to take care of it and be responsible for it. It would not survive unless we gave it water (understanding) and the proper soil (sincerity). It needed sunshine (ability to share), a visit from a bee or butterfly (trustworthiness), and a cultivating hoe (kindness) to break up the ever-hardening ground of indifference.

We arranged these flannel symbols around our flower and, again, we became aware that the absence of one or the other factor had a definite bearing on the health and beauty of our flower. There existed a very practical, vital relationship between my flower and myself--a give and take, a mutual dependence.

We could demonstrate this visually by manipulating our felt symbols--adding and leaving off--but all the time we were talking about things that are invisible: the qualities of friendship. Understanding received and returned; faithfulness accepted and expected; kindness shared and extended; and all the other important components of a friendship are "essential but invisible to the eye, only to be seen rightly with the heart." This was the secret which the fox imparted to the little prince and through him to all of us.

At this point we left the story of the little prince and carried our discussion on friendship one step further. "Our friendships sometimes have to end--my friend moves away, or goes to another school, or dies. But my friendship with God never ends; it is permanent; to Him I am unique in all the world--forever."

> God wants to be friends with me.
> God speaks to me because He loves me.
> He tells me about himself.
> He listens while I tell Him about me.
> Sometimes He just wants to be with me,
>   without words.

And as the children watched, we superimposed the figure of Christ on our flower--"Christ, the source of true friendship, the basis of all love" (Dom Hubert Van Zeller).

So let us continue to use words, but let us also speak in sounds, gestures, movements, and colors. And as we thus expand our being we may find that we are moving into new areas of truth, or perhaps better yet, that we are beginning to see and sense the truth about where we now are.

— Stanford Summers

SOME "NON-RELIGIOUS" BOOKS THAT CAN BE USED
IN TEACHING RELIGION

The following selection of books is by no means definitive--and the suggested applications are only meant as a stimulation for your own imagination, and to give a large enough list to ensure that you will be able to find a good number at your library. Each book has a variety of uses, underlying symbols, and levels of meaning. As you read them, you will see that:

some present more teaching possibilities than others,

some are merely good, others are classics,

some have deeper levels of meaning than others,

some are better for younger children, others are for older children,

and some are good any time and any place,

some will strike a responsibe chord in you, while others will not.

USE AND ENJOY THE ONES THAT DO!

Anglund, Joan Walsh. <u>A Friend Is Someone who Likes You</u>. New York: Harcourt, Brace, Jovanovich, 1958.
The wonder and delight of many kinds of friends.
(friendship, creativity)

Beim, Lorraine & Jerrold. <u>Two Is a Team</u>. New York: Harcourt, Brace, Jovanovich, 1945, 1974.
Team work and friendship of a black and his white friend.
(Christian community and sharing; communal aspect of grace, redemption and church)

Bennett, Rainey. <u>What Do You Think?</u> New York: World.
Tony tries to figure out what thinking is.
(appreciation of power of thinking; our dependence upon experience and people and things for knowledge)

Berger, Terry. <u>Being Alone, Being Together</u>. Chicago: Advanced Learning Concepts/Children's Press, 1974.
It's nice being alone sometimes; it's also nice being with friends sometimes.
(understanding feelings, friendship)

_____. _I Have Feelings_. Morningside Heights, New York: Behavioral
    Publications, 1971.
    Simple and clear presentation of the feelings--positive and negative
    that children experience.
    (understanding feelings, self-acceptance)

Borten, Helen. _A Picture has a Special Look_. New York: Abelard-Schuman, 1961.
    The materials used (pencil, pen, paint, crayon, pastel) change the look
    of a picture, and the feeling that the picture gives the viewer.
    (sensitivity to world around us; uniqueness of each person; appreciation
    of our power of creativity)

Brown, Marcia. _Stone Soup_. New York, Charles Scribner's Sons, 1947 (hardback);
    Scholastic Book Services, 1971 (paper).
    Three soldiers trick selfish villagers into sharing their food, and enjoy-
    ing the celebration.
    (useful as part of a study of hunger; a celebration of sharing--e.g. each
    child brings a vegetable and a "stone soup" is actually made)

Buckley, Helen E. _Grandfather and I_. New York: Lothrop, Lee & Shepard, 1959.
    A small boy loves to walk with his grandfather because everyone else in
    the family goes too fast.
    (each person's unique gift; respect for the aged; family relationships)

_____. _Grandmother and I_. New York: Lothrop, Lee & Shepard, 1961.
    Grandmothers have their own special gift of caring.
    (respect for the aged; family relationships)

Burton, Virginia. _The Little House_. Boston: Houghton-Mifflin, 1942.
    A little house in the country witnesses changes and progress around her.
    (change; growth; life patterns of birth-growth-death-new life)

Eckblad, Edith. _Kindness is a Lot of Things_. Norwalk, Connecticut: Gibson.
    "Kindness is letting someone else feel big. Kindness is . . ."
    (Christian love, kindness, concern; lighthearted but realistic formation
    of conscience for children)

Economakis, Olga. _Oasis of the Stars_. New York: Coward-McCann, 1965.
    Arab boy longs for a real home, but his family must keep moving to find
    water; he digs a well.
    (pilgrim church; values in other cultures; human pattern of death-new
    life; readiness to follow the Spirit; Exodus; baptism; grace)

Estes, Eleanor. _The Hundred Dresses_. New York: Harcourt, Brace, Jovanovich,
    1944.
    Girl is treated as an outsider, brags about her hundred dresses though
    she wears the same one every day.
    (respect for differences, compassion, dealing with "cliques")

Evans, Eva Knox. _All About Us_. New York: Golden Press, 1968.
    Inexpensive paperback discusses racial, cultural & religious differences
    in terms children can appreciate; amusing tone.
    (appreciating diversity)

_____. _People Are Important_. New York: Capitol Publishing Co., 1951.
   Entertaining approach to intergroup understanding on local, national,
   international levels.
   (appreciating diversity; solving problems)

Fern, Eugene. _Pepito's Story_. New York: Farrar, Straus & Giroux, 1960.
   Lonely Spanish boy finds happiness when he aids a sick playmate.
   (love and caring; values in other cultures)

Francoise. _The Thank-You Book_. New York: Charles Scribner's Sons, 1947.
   Picture book in which child thanks all the things that make him happy.
   (sensitivity to and appreciation of world around us)

Gallico, Paul. _The Snow Goose_. New York: Alfred A. Knopf, 1966.
   A crippled bird is the occasion of friendship between a young girl and
   a deformed but loving recluse.
   (the opportunity of grace, love; the Holy Spirit; seeing beneath the
   surface)

Gartner, Joselma & Watry, Dolores. _How Big I Am_. New York: Herder & Herder,
   1968.
   A child's eye view of growing up.
   (self acceptance & identity; celebrating the ordinary expeiriences of life)

Houston, James. _The White Archer: An Eskimo Legend_. New York: Harcourt, Brace
   Jovanovich, 1967.
   Boy bows revenge on Indians who kill his family, finally learns that hatred
   is destructive.
   (sanctity of life; harmony with nature; making decisions; values in other
   cultures)

Kantrowitz, Mildred. _I Wonder if Herbie's Home Yet_. New York: Parents' Magazine Press, 1971.
   A child suffers until a misunderstanding is cleared up.
   (human relationships; community)

Kirn, Ann. _Two Pesos For Catalina_. Englewood Cliffs, New Jersey: Scholastic
   Book Services, 1969.
   Intense joy of having two pesos and the pleasure of new shoes.
   (parables of lost coin, pearl of great price, hidden treasure; grace; the
   kingdom; values in other cultures)

Krauss, Ruth. _The Growing Story_. New York: Harper-Row, 1947.
   A boy watches things grow, but doesn't realize until fall that he, too,
   has grown.
   (appreciation of our power of growth; change)

Lamorisse, A. _The Red Balloon_. New York: Doubleday, 1947.
   A boy and a balloon become friends; the balloon is not allowed in school,
   at home, or in church; boys try to steal and kill it; all the balloons of
   Paris come to the bereaved boy; he flies away with them.
   (grace; pearl of great price; friendship; redemption)

156

Leaf, Munro. The Story of Ferdinand. New York: Viking, 1936.
    The fortunes of a bull who doesn't want to fight in the ring.
    (pacifism; uniqueness of the individual; integrity)

Lionni, Leo. The Alphabet Tree. New York: Pantheon, 1968.
    Letters become words, words become sentences, sentences say something im-
    portant.
    (meaning of "Word"; the discover of word in flesh; the hope of new words
    which say important things)

_____. Frederick. New York: Pantheon, 1966.
    Mice gather food to prepare for winter, Frederick gathers only colors &
    sunshine, is able to share them when the food gives out.
    (not by bread alone. . . ; respect for differences; uniqueness of each
    person's gift; preoccupation with material goods)

_____. Little Blue and Little Yellow. New York: Astor-Honor, 1959.
    Little Blue and Little Yellow become friends, come to be so close that
    they become green and no one recognizes them.
    (Christian love is transforming; grace; becoming like those we love; com-
    munity)

_____. Swimmy. New York: Pantheon, 1963.
    A small fish helps the others escape from fear and hiding through working
    together.
    (church, community; leadership; Savior)

McCloskey, Robert. Time of Wonder. New York: Viking, 1972.
    Wonders of nature on a beautiful island--seas, storms, hurricane.
    (praise of God through creation; sensitivity to beauty around us)

McGovern, Ann. Who Has A Secret? Boston: Houghton-Mifflin.
    The earth, the night, the clouds, etc. have a secret--burrowing animals,
    stars, rain, etc.
    (God has a secret--love; you have a secret--grace; Christ is our secret,
    etc.; seeing beyond the surface)

Meyer, Renate. Vicki. New York: Atheneum, 1969.
    A girl is ignored, taunted, rejected; the reader supplies most of the
    story; very expressive illustrations.
    (dealing with school "cliques"; respect for differences; handling diffi-
    cult situations)

Miska, Miles. Annie and the Old One. Boston: Little, Brown, 1971.
    Annie learns about death, and why her grandmother had to return to the
    earth.
    (death; respect for the aged; values in other cultures)

Nelson, Lee. All the Sounds We Hear. Austin: Steck-Vaughan.
    Happy sounds, sad sounds, all the sounds in our world.
    (appreciation of power of hearing; sensitivity to beauty & wonders around
    us; hearing God's Word spoken through people and events in everyday life)

Ness, Evaline. Do You Have the Time, Lydia? New York: Dutton, 1971.
    A girl is too selfish to help her brother, but learns to take the time
    for others.
    (caring and sharing; community; family relationships)

O'Neill, Mary. Hailstones and Halibut Bones. Garden City, New York: Doubleday,
    1961.
    Poems listing people, objects, places & feelings suggested by each color.
    (sensitivity to beauty & to the world around us; appreciation of power
    of sight)

Piatti, Celestino. The Happy Owls. New York: Atheneum, 1964.
    Barnyard animals ask the owls the secret of their happiness but can't
    understand the wisdom of the reply, and return to their quarrels.
    (appreciation of the possibilities in each life; joy; unity; seeing beyond
    the surface of things; relationship of war and selfishness, peace and
    contentment)

Pintoff, Ernest. Always Help a Bird (Especially With a Broken Leg).
    New York: Harper-Row, 1965.
    A boy and girl rescue a bird and help fix his leg.
    (Christian caring; joy)

Price, Christine. Happy Days. New York: United States Committe for UNICEF,
    1969.
    Ways of celebrating birth, birthday & name-days around the world.
    (appreciating diversity; celebration/liturgy)

Rand, Ann & Paul. I Know a Lot of Things. New York: Harcourt, Brace, Jovano-
    vich, 1956.
    List of things a young child would realize that he knows.
    (appreciation of the power of thought; growth)

_____. Sparkle and Spin: A Book About Words. New York: Harper-Row, 1957.
    Noticing words.
    (appreciation of language and communication; symbols which communicate--
    sacrament; God's Word)

de St.-Exupery, Antoine. The Little Prince. New York: Harcourt, Brace, Jovano-
    vich, 1943, 1966.
    Travels of a little prince, meetings with animals & people with all-too-
    human characteristics, his love of a flower, his friendship with a fox,
    his effect upon the author. A classic!!
    (each episode has many possibilities)

Seuss, Dr. The Sneetches and Other Stories. New York: Random House, 1961.
    Proud & unhappy animals trying to make themselves better than others.
    (prejudice & discrimination; pharisaism; snobbery of any sort)

Silverstein, Shel. The Giving Tree. New York: Harper-Row, 1964.
    A tree loves a boy, and gives him apples, branches, and trunk--though the
    boy is ungrateful, the tree continues to give.
    (Christian love)

Smith, Garry. Flagon The Dragon. Austin: Steck-Vaughan.
Unhappy dragon eventually finds his place in the world.
(uniqueness of each person; vocation; talents)

Stinetorf, Louisa. A Charm for Paco's Mother. New York: John Day, 1965.
Boy notices the needs of many persons and animals on his way to pray at
the great stone cross on Christmas eve.
(caring, compassion)

Tresselt, Alvin. The Frog in the Well. New York: Lothrop, Lee & Shephard,
1958.
The frog who thought his well was the whole world, found out the truth.
(human tendency toward narrowness; growth; openness)

_____. Wake Up City! New York: Lothrop, Lee, & Shephard, 1957.
The gradual awakening of the city, from earliest paling of the stars.
For the very young.
(sensitivity to world around us; community of people/church; gradual
awakening to God's love)

Udry, Janice May. A Tree Is Nice. New York: Harper-Row, 1956.
Many delights to be had in, with or under a tree.
(appreciation of the world around us; tree as symbol of God/church)

_____. Let's Be Enemies. New York: Harper-Row, 1961.
Realistic yet lighthearted presentation of friends who break up and make
up.
(human relationships; handling difficult situations)

Ungerer, Tomi. The Three Robbers. New York: Atheneum, 1975.
Whimsical story in which a child shows three robbers how to use their
treasure to help others.
(hidden talents, community, sharing, cooperation)

Viorst, Judith. The Tenth Good Thing About Barney. New York: Atheneum, 1971.
Young boy deals with the death of his pet cat.
(death education; handling difficult situations; family sharing)

White, E. B. Charlotte's Web. New York: Harper-Row, 1952.
Spider uses her creativity to help her friend the pig. A classic!!
(friendship, creativity; death)

Williams, Margery. The Velveteen Rabbit. New York: Doubleday, 1958.
A toy becomes real when it is loved.
(caring friendship; family relationship)

Wojciechowska, Maia. Shadow of a Bull. New York: Atheneum, 1966.
Son of a great bullfighter lacks courage and will to fight; must make
a decision between his desires and expectations of the community.
(handling difficult situations; integrity; uniqueness of each person)

Zolotow, Charlotte. <u>The Hating Book</u>. New York: Harper-Row, 1969.
_____.   <u>The Quarreling Book</u>. New York: Harper-Row, 1963.
_____.   <u>The Unfriendly Book</u>. New York: Harper-Row, 1975.
    Children confronted with the common experiences and problems of life.
    Lighthearted approach.
    (human relationships; friendship; community; dealing with difficulties)

BOOKS (AND ARTICLES) ABOUT BOOKS

"Aids in the Selection of Materials for Children and Young Adults," Chicago:
    American Library Association. A free pamphlet.

Arbuthnot, Mary Hill. <u>Children and Books</u>. Glenview, Illinois: Scott, Fores-
    man, 1964.

"Brotherhood Books," bibliography for all age children. Reprint of <u>St. Joseph</u>
    <u>Magazine</u>, March 1967. Needs to be up-dated, but a good beginning.

Eakin, Mary K. <u>Good Books for Children</u>. Chicago: University of Chicago Press,
    1962.

<u>Human Values in Children's Literature</u>. New York: Interracial Council on Books
    for Children.

Gillespie, John & Lembo, Diana. <u>Introducing Books: A Guide for the Middle</u>
    <u>Grades</u>. New York: R. R. Bowker Co., 1970.

Griffin, Louise. <u>Multi-Ethnic Books for Young Children</u>. Washington, D.C.:
    Eric-NAEYC/National Association for the Education of Young Children, n.d.

Keating, Charlotte Matthews. <u>Building Bridges of Understanding Between Cultures</u>.
    Tucson: Palo Verde Publishing Co., 1971.

Kircher, Clara. <u>Behavior Patterns in Children's Books</u>. Washington, D.C.: Ca-
    tholic University of America Press, 1966.

Sawyer, Ruth. <u>The Way of the Storyteller</u>. New York: Viking Press, 1962.

BIBLIOGRAPHY

The following lists of books and other resources have been included in this book:

Many of the books mentioned in these lists contain excellent bibliographies. Professional journals of education and religious education are also a valuable resource. The following books and articles, which do not fit into any of the other lists in this book, or which cover several areas of activity, are well worth your attention:

Audio-Visual Resource Guide for Use in Religious
        Education. Department of A-V and Broadcast
        Education of National Council of Churches
        of Christ in USA, 475 Riverside Drive, New
        York, New York 10027, 1965.

Children's Liturgies. ed. Virginia Sloyan & Gabe
        Huck. Washington, D.C.: The Liturgical Con-
        ference, 1970. Chapters on music; art;
        stories, poems & drama; movement & dance;
        et. al.

Flemming, Bonnie Mack, Hamilton, Darlene Softley and Hicks, Joanne Deal. Re-
        sources for Creative Teaching in Early Childhood Education. New York:
        Harcourt, Brace, Jovanovich, 1977. Earlier editions of this excellent
        curriculum guide were published by the Kansas Association for the Edu-
        cation of Young Children.

Goodwin, Mary T. & Pollen, Gerry. <u>Creative Food Experiences for Children</u>. Washington, D.C.: Center for Science in the Public Interest, 1974.

Heffernan, Helen & Burton, William. <u>The Step Beyond: Creativity</u>. Washington, D.C.: National Education Association, 1964.

Jeep, Elizabeth McMahon. <u>Exchange</u>. Cincinnati: CEBCO/Pflaum, 1974. A "CATECHIST" Collection.

_____, and Huck, Gabe. <u>Celebrate Summer! A Guidebook for Families</u>, and <u>Celebrate Summer! A Guidebook for Congregations</u>. New York: Paulist Press, 1973.

Mattox, Beverly A. <u>Getting It Together: Dilemmas for the Classroom Based on Kohlberg's Approach</u>. San Diego: Pennant Press, 1975.

Mearns, Hughes. <u>Creative Power</u>. 2nd Ed. Rev. New York: Dover Publications, 1958.

<u>Parishes and Families</u>. Edited by Gabe Huck & Virginia Sloyan. Washington, D.C.: The Liturgical Conference, 1976.

<u>Signs, Songs and Stories: Another Look at Children's Liturgies</u>. Edited by Virginia Sloyan. Washington, D.C.: The Liturgical Conference, 1974. Chapters on prayer; music; mime, improvisation & dance; et. al.

Schreivogel, Paul. <u>The World of Art--The World of Youth; A Primer on the Use of Arts in Youth Ministry</u>. Minneapolis: Augsburg, 1968.

Wittich, Walter A. and Schuller, Charles F. <u>Audiovisual Materials: Their Nature and Use</u>. 3rd edition. New York: Harper, 1962.